"This book is dedicated to my canine companion, Jordan, who displayed in his own unique way what it means to be Souled Out unconditionally. In spite of the challenges you encountered, for almost 17 years you gave Jan and me your unconditional love. Your place in my heart is unparalleled."

Why I'm
Souled Out

The Chronology of My Experiences

Why I'm
Souled Out
The Chronology of My Experiences

Reverend Gregory L. Williamson

Editors
Ray Glandon
Kimberly Williams

ASA PUBLISHING CORPORATION
AN INNOVATIVE OUTSOURCE BOOK PUBLISHING HYBRID

ASA Publishing Corporation
1285 N. Telegraph Rd., #376, Monroe, Michigan 48162
An Accredited Publishing House with the BBB
www.asapublishingcorporation.com

All Rights Reserved. No part of this publication may be reproduced, stored in a retrieval system or transmitted in any form or by any means electronic, mechanical, photocopying, recording or otherwise, without the prior written permission of the publisher. Author/writer rights to "Freedom of Speech" protected by and with the "1st Amendment" of the Constitution of the United States of America. This is a work of non-fiction Christian education. Any resemblance to actual events, locales, person living or deceased that is not related to the author's literacy is entirely coincidental.

With this title/copyrights page, the reader is notified that the publisher does not assume, and expressly disclaims any obligation to obtain and/or include any other information other than that provided by the author except with permission. Any belief system, promotional motivations, including but not limited to the use of non-fictional/fictional characters and/or characteristics of this book, are within the boundaries of the author's own creativity in order to reflect the nature and concept of the book. Unless otherwise indicated, all scripture quotations are taken from the various bibles in accordance to the author's Appendix within this book.

Any and all vending sales and distribution not permitted without full book cover and this copyrights page.

Copyrights©2020 Reverend Gregory L. Williamson, All Rights Reserved
Book Title: Why I'm Souled Out *The Chronology of My Experiences*
Date Published: 06.15.2020 / Edition 1 *Trade Paperback*
Book ID: ASAPCID2380806
ISBN: 978-1-946746-77-1
Library of Congress Cataloging-in-Publication Data

This book was published in the United States of America.
Great State of Michigan

Table of Contents

Introduction		1
Chapter 1	Our Divine Purpose	9
Chapter 2	An Angel at the Door	17
Chapter 3	The Call to Preach	25
Chapter 4	An Electrifying Experience	35
Chapter 5	The Drum and the Real Estate Deal	43
Chapter 6	A Quiet Place	53
Chapter 7	Make You To Become	63
Chapter 8	A Balancing Act	71
Chapter 9	Helicopters and Airplanes	83
Chapter 10	Processing It All	93
Chapter 11	It's all about the Journey	103
Chapter 12	Souled Out	117
Acknowledgements		139
Appendix		143

Why I'm
Souled Out

The Chronology of My Experiences

Reverend Gregory L. Williamson

Introduction

The Word of God is the roadmap that provides direction for believers as they journey through life. Moreover, it is the assurance we rely on to transport us to eternal life with our Savior. God creates within each believer a unique purpose. Once it is discovered and acted upon, a series of events take place with the intention of building character, faith, and boldness.

The Bible is replete with examples: Abel, Noah, Abraham, Isaac, Jacob, Joseph, Moses, Joshua, Caleb, Ruth, Hannah, Samuel, Esther, all of the prophets and judges, and more. In the New Testament, we have countless examples of faith and boldness, but none compares to the likes of John the Baptist, Jesus, and His disciples. Today, God is seeking the same level of faith and boldness from His followers. Jesus is our most challenging example, but He is also our best example. Remember His words at *John 14:12*,

"Verily, verily, I say unto you, He that believeth on me, the works that I do shall he do also; and greater works than these shall he do; because I go unto my Father."

These works, for all intents and purposes, will not be "greater than" the works Jesus performed. They can be "greater" in number, however, because we are greater in number. So why is this not happening in greater numbers?

Fear and ignorance are two of the greatest impediments for followers of Christ. Someone defined fear as **F**alse **E**xpectations **A**ppearing **R**eal. Fear is a real emotion; however, what's being feared is said to almost never occur. Fear can also be healthy. Often times fear prevents or dissuades us from doing ourselves harm. Fear can be good or bad, based on the way it is managed.

Ignorance is not a nasty word. It is not a demeaning word. It's simply a word that reveals our lack of knowledge in a particular area. Shakespeare wrote, "There is no ignorance but darkness." Ignorance just means that we are in the dark in some situations. God does not want us to walk in fear or ignorance. He doesn't want us walking in darkness either. John 8:12 records these words from our Lord,

Jesus spoke again unto them, saying, "I am the light of the world: he that follows me shall not walk in darkness, but shall have the light of life."

God prefers a loving and intimate relationship with us. He explains that at I John 4:18:

"There is no fear in love; but perfect love casts out fear: because fear hath torment. He that fears is not made perfect in love."

Fear and faith cannot occupy the same space at the same time. That's where knowledge and ignorance come into the equation. Ignorance says, "I can't do this." Godly Knowledge says, "*I can do all things through Christ, who strengthens me.*" Our confident, assuring answer is always in the Word of God. Paul says at II *Corinthians 2:11, Lest Satan should get an advantage of us: for we are not ignorant of his devices.* We must know and remember, *the battle is not ours, it's the Lords* - I Samuel 17:47.

The goal of this book is not to produce perfect people. It is, however, intended to provide building blocks and a pathway to a perfect love relationship with God. Through that relationship of trust, God will produce perfect results. The world around us is constantly changing. God's message is consistent, but the manner in which it is administered is ever-changing.

A large part of that process necessitates an acceptance to change. As our churches (the body of believers, not the building) are growing older, they are not being replenished with younger disciples. Part of the reason is relevancy. If the church is going to appeal to the younger generation, we must be willing to change our methods in reaching them.

I have been so encouraged by the creative methods that young ministries are using to reach out to the younger population. Pastors Keon Henderson, Chris Sands, JaMichael Jordan, and Lakweshia Ewing are just a few of the younger, up and coming ministers that have placed greater emphasis on reaching the younger generation. Much of their success is predicated on their willingness to change. They are not compromising the message; they are creatively revamping their methods.

One person or a few ministries are not going to bring about these necessary changes. However, investigating what others are doing that's yielding positive and constructive results can open the minds of other church leaders to pursue new ideas as God directs. Chris and Lakweshia are involved in an initiative called "We, Over Me." I am very optimistic about its message and the potential it promotes.

Until we understand that a "we" mentality accomplishes more than an "I" mentality, we will continue to struggle individually. What excites me most about the work of these younger disciples is the realization that the earlier these younger disciples are motivated, the more time and energy they will have to make a difference. I thank God for my souled out relationship with Him, but I wish I had encountered Him in this intimate way sooner in life. *(Google their names to see what they are doing).*

I have always believed that when we take care of our seniors and our youth, it will be reimbursed. It is a shame to see such a rich and blessed country as ours being outclassed by poorer countries in the treatment and care of their seniors and youth. We have intelligent, influential young people today who are very capable of making changes for the better. That's one reason I favor the idea of utilizing younger men in their twenty's to fifty's, to take on the more challenging roles in kingdom building.

While saving lives is God's work, He uses disciples like us to assist Him. Our approach can yield addition or multiplication. When one woman or one child is saved, one woman or one child's life is changed. When one man is saved, often times, an entire family is changed. Saving lives is what we are called to do, but saving families accomplishes that objective in a more productive manner. God holds men accountable for heading their households, but too often, the male role is subverted. Significant effort needs to be placed on developing within them the necessary qualities to fulfill that responsibility.

I was blessed to be given an opportunity to organize a Men's conference in Michigan for 12 years. From that endeavor, I witnessed countless numbers of men whose lives were completely transformed. As a result, their families were impacted as well. Equally beneficial, the church families that they were a part of began to see change. God likes addition, but He loves multiplication. After all, that was His command from the beginning. At Genesis 1:28 & 9:1, God instructed us to – *"Be fruitful and multiply."*

Well, that's where I am, and that's where you can be as well. I continue to work with men, and I am encouraged by the results. I love working with seniors, it's my way of thanking God for the men of God that He placed around my mother during her senior years. I still get excited when working with youth. That affords me the opportunity to share my mistakes, my humanness, my defiance, and more importantly, God's forgiveness.

I am not the product of an affluent upbringing, but I was raised by two parents that exposed me to God and the church. From that experience I developed priorities (Matthew 6:33). I learned time management (Ecclesiastes 3). I acquired peace of mind (Philippians 4:7). I eventually developed an intimate relationship with God (I John 2:5). I am productively involved in kingdom building (Luke 18:16).

I had the ultimate opportunity last year to visit the Holy Land, and nothing solidified my relationship like that experience. Seeing in person what I have read in scripture was amazing. Most importantly, my life has even more significance and purpose (Matthew 28:19-20).

In the most relevant and compelling way I can, let me say this, I am for sure no anomaly. If God can develop a souled out relationship with me, He can certainly do the same with you. I understand that there are economic, social, political, cultural, and religious obstacles that impact our decision-making. I understand that the playing field is not always level. In fact, it may never be level. God, however, plumbs where He stands. Right now, He stands with arms open and hands extended, waiting on you to completely submit your life unto Him. He wants to do extraordinary things through you, not just for you but for every life your journey touches. Don't delay. Don't allow Satan an opportunity to negatively impact your thinking. Make that commitment right now to be Souled Out for the Lord. In Jesus Name, Amen.

Chapter 1 - Our Divine Purpose

"But from there, you will search for the LORD your God, and you will find Him when you seek Him with all your heart and all your soul." Deuteronomy 4:29

Have you ever reflected on your personal talents and gifts? I mean, do you ever think about the various interests you have and why they appeal to you. Some of them may be external in nature, such as cooking, sewing, wood-working, painting, athletic skills, speaking, or a host of other physical skills and abilities that seem to come naturally.

There are others, however, that are more internal in nature, such as motivating and encouraging others or assisting others in fulfilling their interests and desires. It might be working with children or seniors or caring for those with medical challenges. While we often take these skills for granted or perceive them to be innate, they are more likely God-given gifts, talents, and abilities.

Do you notice that when you exercise these skills, you seem to come alive and become energized? Not everyone can motivate others with words or an ability to just listen. Have you ever wondered about the times when you build or design something that others rave over and you look at them in awe, wondering, "What's the big deal?" Well, it is a big deal because God has poured into you and all of us talents and skills that might be thought of as just natural to the naked eye, but they're really supernatural.

Periodically, take a little time to make a list of activities and matters that not only interest you but also you seem to excel in. Ask yourself, "What's the one thing that I seem to do better than others?" This might be introspection into your God-given purpose.

The gifts God gives are like little seeds planted inside us. These seeds, however, must be nurtured and developed. This nurturing comes about through our everyday experiences associated with them. In the right environment, these seeds flourish, grow, and develop. In the wrong environment, these seeds often wither and die. That's just one salient reason why we have to be careful about the people we allow into the innermost parts of our lives.

If our seeds are to grow and become productively and constructively effective, we have to use them. We must identify which "Gift Seeds" God has given us. Sometimes, these God-given seeds can be identified by pursuing the things that we are most interested in. Through these experiences, God will reveal more about whom we are and how He has called us to serve Him.

The Bible is replete with examples of people that God endowed with unique abilities. As they utilized them, He displayed His omnipotent power through them, to encourage others, develop the person using them, and to bring glory to Himself.

God has called you to a purpose, and He wants you to walk in it for others and for yourself. In doing this, we experience the personal peace and joy that Apostle Paul expressed at Romans 15:13 – *"I pray that God, the source of all hope, will infuse your lives with an abundance of joy and peace in the midst of your faith so that your hope will overflow through the power of the Holy Spirit"* and at Philippians 4:7 – *"And the peace of God, which passeth all understanding, shall keep your hearts and minds through Christ Jesus."*

Yes, God has called you unto Himself for a special and unique purpose. He is completely able to reveal your purpose to you, and He will, as you listen to Him and diligently seek Him (Revelation 2:7 & Heb. 11:6).

So, how do we hear Him and seek Him that we cannot see? We must remember that God is Spirit, and we must seek Him and worship Him in spirit and truth (John 4:24). Although you probably won't hear an audible sound when God is speaking to you, there are audible messages that you can receive. Those will often come from other messengers, some internal and some external.

As we have discussed earlier, He often speaks to our ears through our hearts. The gifts, talents, and passions you have are not by accident or coincidental. God stirs your heart through those mediums. While we listen to them, we don't become controlled or guided by them. They simply aid us in discovering the heart of God.

If we focus totally on our gifts, talents, and passions without the spiritual guidance of the Holy Spirit, we can fall prey to selfishness, arrogance, pride, and even narcissism. Think of a diverse group of talented (famous) people with whom you are familiar. Now drill down into their personal lives and you will find that some of them are only concerned with their own celebrity. If the category is sports, you will find some that are only concerned with their stats at the expense of the team's success. There is another group, although usually smaller in number that is equally committed to their craft but the success that comes as a result of it is shared in civic and community endeavors.

This latter group not only listens to their gifts, talents, and passions but they also listen to their inner spirit. Their heart for God and the maturity that develops in those that listen to the voice of God reveals the real meaning of success. They have seen the temporary realities of material possessions. They have seen, and in many instances, experienced the discomfort and dissatisfaction that often accompany that pursuit. They have learned to listen to and respond differently because those pursuits usually produce negative yield.

Too many of us have been taught from our early years that pain, suffering, discomfort, struggle, disappointment, dissatisfaction, and other uncomfortable challenges in our life are signs of God using us and Satan warring against us because of it. While true in some instances, more often than not, we are the perpetrator of our discomfort.

Without a doubt, God allows opposition to come against us and when He does, it is intended to strengthen us. Many times we're not strengthened because we are not spiritually mature enough to properly deal with it. I don't mean to ignore our limited ability, but that's exactly what we have to do in these situations. When we recognize that we are limited *in our own strength but unlimited in Christ,* we are then able to slay these giants.

"I have strength for all things through Christ, who empowers me."
Philippians 4:13

Notwithstanding, I have learned through experience the real meaning of a statement one of my Deans used to convey to us, relative to the concept of struggle. As he reminded us that God allows struggle and its intent is to grow and develop us, we must stay connected in relationship with Him because *"Struggles will strengthen us, if they don't crush us."*

So, yes, struggles can be a result of spiritual warfare and an indication that God wants to move you to another area of purpose, ministry, or level of effectiveness in your spiritual pursuit. One very important factor to always keep in mind is that you are just one individual and sometimes our answer is beyond our personal comprehension.

"A wise man will hear, and will increase learning; because a man of understanding shall attain unto wise counsels:"
Proverbs 1:5

All of us should have spiritually mature mentors or accountability partners with whom we share our concerns, pursuits, and struggles. These people are not loosely discovered. Sharing your innermost matters with uncommitted believers can be destructive and sometimes cause more damage than you can repair.

Accountability partners are relationships that develop over time, and they are confirmed by the spirit of God. These relationships have often become the most valuable and useful tools in a disciple's toolbox. Solomon, one of the wisest men in the Bible, warned us at Proverbs 12:15 - **A foolish person is in love with his own opinion, but wisdom means being teachable.**

Every follower of Christ should always have two objectives as they traverse along their journey:

1. There should be someone in their life that has more experience and wisdom pouring into their life.
2. There should be someone with less experience and maturity that they are pouring into.

I speak to these two objectives, not these two people because you might be fortunate enough to have several people pouring into your life or that you are pouring into. Don't limit yourself to one each. Keep in mind that in many instances you will be hard-pressed to find one really committed individual in either category. The main point is – Don't Trust Your Own Judgement independent of counsel from others that have valuable experiences that can free you from unnecessary hardship.

I've had my share of disappointments deriving from dissatisfaction with various outcomes. I've even misattributed the reason for the uncomfortable outcomes to spiritual warfare and haters, but when the dust settled, I could see signs that I overlooked as well as counsel that I ignored. The result: Poor decisions made when my inner-spirit was telling me otherwise.

I fully understand and want you to understand that there will be times when we will struggle against spiritual warfare (Eph. 6:10-12) and that outside counsel is not necessarily advantageous just because it is outside or another opinion. It is beneficial when mixed with and coming from a scriptural and spiritual counselor.

Sometimes, God makes us unsuccessful and/or uncomfortable in situations to move us from those situations. As one writer put it, *"God might be using the discomfort in a lake to move us to an ocean where our gifts can shine."* God will never make you uncomfortable just for discomfort sake.

Yes, dissatisfaction can be a road sign from God to reveal your purpose. Yes, listening to others that confirm your gifting can do the same as well. So, when a brother or sister in Christ notices or comments on one of your talents or gifts don't make light of it. God may be trying to tell you something through those people.

There are times, however, when we shouldn't listen to what others say. There is nothing constructive that comes from negative, condescending, and destructive conversation and advice. But, when someone's counsel agrees with our passions, our internal convictions, our gifting, and what God has already revealed to us personally, it can be a genuine indication of our God-given purpose.

Lastly, in conjunction with all that has been said, we add power to all of these recommendations when we mix them with prayer. It is prayer and communication with our Lord that will invoke the guidance, teaching, and application through the power of the Holy Spirit for purpose and effectiveness.

Ask God to show you the things that move you. Then make a list. He wants you to discover His purpose for you more than you do. Your purpose is not just about you; it's about what God wants to do through you. Don't ignore or neglect the dissatisfaction you feel when others deny your gifts and your passions. If you do, you are not only betraying yourself, you are betraying God because He has called you to a purpose. He wants you to walk in it for the edification of others and for your own joy, peace, and assurance.

Chapter 2 - An Angel At The Door

"I am now going the way of all the earth, and you know with all your heart and all your soul that none of the good promises the Lord your God made to you has failed. Everything was fulfilled for you; not one promise has failed." Joshua 23:14

Throughout biblical history, God has shown Himself as a priest, provider, and protector in various ways. One of those ways has been by way of dispensing angels to provide protection and direction. While they may not appear in ways that we understand angels, they show up in our lives at times when no one else could meet our needs. The writer of Hebrews reminds us to be aware of this in our daily encounters.

"Don't forget to extend your hospitality to all—even to strangers—for as you know, some have unknowingly shown kindness to heavenly messengers in this way." Hebrews 13:2

The message above alerts us to the reality that while we sometimes take little thought about whom we are interacting with on occasion, God has orchestrated our lives in such a way that He will often dispatch angels to protect and assist us in fulfilling our purpose and accomplishing His will.

At Genesis 19:5, we find an example of just that. The Word of God says - ᴬᵗ *dawn, the heavenly messengers urged Lot to action again. Lot, you need to get up and take your wife and two daughters out of here. Otherwise, you will be consumed along with the rest of the city.*

If you are familiar with the story, you know that Abraham gave Lot the opportunity to choose where he and his family would reside, and he chose Sodom. God decided to destroy Sodom; not arbitrarily and not without extending great mercy and consideration.

If you look back in Chapter 18, you will find Abraham pleading with God to spare the city for the sake of the righteous living in Sodom. The conversation ends when God reveals that there are not even 10 righteous residing in Sodom. Nevertheless, God dispatches angels to Sodom to save Lot and his family from this great destruction that is about to occur.

Maybe you are more familiar with Jacob's experience. Genesis 28:11-12 says, *Jacob dreamed: A stairway was set on the ground with its top reaching heaven, and God's angels were going up and down on it. ¹³ Yahweh was standing there beside him, saying, "I am Yahweh, the God of your father Abraham and the God of Isaac. I will give you and your offspring the land that you are now sleeping on.* In Verse 16 we read - *When Jacob awoke from his sleep, he said, "Surely the LORD is in this place, and I did not know it."*

Allow me to give one more example. When Jesus was about to be betrayed and taken by the Roman soldiers, (Matthew 26) Peter drew his sword striking one of the soldiers. In Verses 52 and 53, *Jesus told him, "Put your sword back in its place because all who take up a sword will perish by a sword. Or do you think that I cannot call on My Father, and He will provide Me at once with more than 12 legions of angels?*

These are just a few examples of proof that God can and does (when He chooses to) dispatch angels on our behalf to accomplish His will. Not to mention the occasions when we are assisted and are not even aware of it. So, now that the stage has been set, let me share a personal story with you that my mother shared with me.

I was raised with both parents in my home. I had 7 siblings. I was the fourth born of eight, and the three siblings born before me were boys. One day when I was about a year old, I was in the kitchen crawling around, and my mother was in the next room folding clothes she had washed. Almost simultaneously, the doorbell rang and I began crying uncontrollably.

The two had no connection. It wasn't like I cried when the doorbell rang. I was just told that the two occurred together. My mother ran into the kitchen, picked me up, and preceded to the front door. There was a man she didn't know so she inquired about his reason for ringing the bell. I was still crying. The man said he was sent to the house because there was a problem. My mother told him there were no problems. We were the only ones home at the time. The man repeated that he was sent because there was a problem. My mother repeated, *"There is no problem here."* The man then said, what's wrong with the child?

My mother said, I don't know. He was in the kitchen and as the doorbell rang, he started to cry. She began to look me over to see if I was hurt in some way that she had overlooked. She found nothing. The man said, let me have him. I don't know why she gave me to him, a man she didn't even know, but she did.

The man took me in his arms, began to rock me and talk to me, and for whatever reason, she said I stopped crying. He then asked if it was okay if he prayed for me. She said sure. He prayed and then handed me back over to my mother. My mother took me, turned around, and put me down on the floor. When she raised up and turned back to the door, the man was gone.

My mother ran to the porch door, looked all around, but could not see anyone in any direction. No car, no one walking, no one in sight. Other than my father, she shared this story with no one for years.

Around age 4, I began writing out sermons (copying scriptures) from the Bible. I would go around the house reading these messages to anyone that would listen. My father and mother had a discussion with our church Pastor about what I was doing.

They also told him the story about the man that came to the door years prior.

They collectively believed that the man was an angel or messenger from God and that he was sent there that day to anoint me. Please keep in mind that I am only the messenger conveying to you what was told to me many years later. I wish I could tell you that after that event, I lived the life of a saint, preaching Gospel messages as a child, traveling around the country healing the sick and was instrumental in restoring, encouraging, and changing lives. That, however, was not the case.

I was raised in the church, as were all of my siblings, and our church experience had a huge impact on each of our lives. In spite of the many wrongs we all committed, there were some things that our conscience just would not allow us to do. Nevertheless, over the course of the next 13 years, my habits, behavior, and practices were not reflective of the first 4 years of my life.

Looking back, I understand why it is so vitally important that parents provide as much guidance and protection for their children as possible. Even those parents that do, can't, always prevent their children from going astray. As youngsters and teens, we really think we know it all, at least as much as we need to do what we want, until we find ourselves in trouble.

At age 17, I moved out. I didn't move into my own place; I rented a room in my brother's apartment. I was still in high school, my car was paid for, and I had a job at Sears that paid me enough to cover rent, gas, and food as long as nothing went wrong. You've probably already figured out that "something went wrong." I let someone drive my car. He damaged it, couldn't afford to fix it, and when I did, my budget was so challenged, I could never catch up.

I didn't understand the intrinsic depth of John 10:10. When John said that Satan comes only but to steal, kill, and destroy, I didn't realize just how crafty and committed he is. He cleverly enticed me with various material things, people, and opportunities until a distance developed between those things to which I was so committed, only to replace them with other interests. But, Satan would not win this battle.

There is a passage of scripture in the book of Philippians that I rest in today. Oh how I wish I had been more familiar with it then.

"Being confident of this very thing, that he which hath begun a good work in you will perform it until the day of Jesus Christ:"
Philippians 1:6

Paul's words here, provide assurance for me and you that when God has His hand on your life, He doesn't give up or give in. He gives us free will, yet determines how far we slide before we come to our senses and realize that what we are doing or the road we are traveling is only going to end in destruction. Luke writes about a similar situation in the 15th Chapter of the Gospel of Luke.

Verses 17-20 says - *"When he came to his senses, He said; 'All those farmhands working for my father sit down to three meals a day, and here I am starving to death. I'm going back to my father. I'll say to him, Father, I've sinned against God, I've sinned before you; I don't deserve to be called your son. Take me on as a hired hand.' He got right up and went home to his father."*

Well, I didn't have an inheritance to leave with, and I didn't find myself in a famine-like situation. I did, however, find myself sinking and in a situation that was over my head. I thank God that He is a kind and compassionate Father. I also thank God for giving me a kind and compassionate earthly father. When I decided that I had no choice but to go to my father and ask if I could come back home, I never had to utter those words. He simply said to me: *"You can't make it out there, can you?"* It was so much easier for me to answer his question than it would have been to tell him how I had failed.

In one year, I had recovered: bills paid off, a better vehicle, and a new job that paid 3 times as much as Sears did. I had become more active in the church, and life was great. *I could afford to move again.*

Chapter 3 - The Call to Preach

"Here is My Servant whom I have chosen, My beloved in whom My soul delights; I will put My Spirit on Him, and He will proclaim justice to the nations." Matthew 12:18

Too often, Disciples of Christ confuse or misconstrue a personal unction from the Holy Spirit to be a "calling" into the gospel ministry. God does call ministers into the preaching of the gospel by way of the Holy Spirit, but He also uses that same Holy Spirit in calling His people to all aspects of ministry.

"Before I even formed you in your mother's womb, I knew all about you. Before you drew your first breath, I had already chosen you to be My prophet to speak My word to the nations." Jeremiah 1:5

Sometimes it is not the preaching ministry that calls us. There are a vast number of essentials that aid in producing, organizing, and administrating the various aspects of fulfilling the completeness of the gospel ministry. Paul instructs us with these words, **"For just as we have many parts in one body—and all the parts do not have the same function—so we, who are many, are**

one body in The Messiah and everyone parts of one another. We have gifts that differ according to the grace that was given to us— if prophecy, in proportion to our faith; ^{if} service, in our serving; or the one who teaches, in his teaching;" Romans 12:4-7

Whether the calling comes before or after accepting Christ as personal Savior, we all find ourselves in places that are not conducive to our God-given purpose. When this occurs, God, at some point, in His own way, will utilize the characteristics of the Holy Spirit to speak to us.

If your gifting and purpose is in the area of serving, that does not involve traditional or specific preaching of the gospel, the pull on your life will nevertheless feel the same. These are the times when we should seek, submit, and surrender ourselves to Him fully. He will then, through a course of actions that He deems appropriate, begin to show or reveal that for which you are being called.

There are so many men and women of God that were poorly counseled or in many instances, not counseled at all, and they feel trapped in a ministry for which they were not called. Their perceived embarrassment of admitting or revealing a sense of entrapment drives many of them to continue on a road that is productive, but seriously lacking significance.

We will be most effective when we are operating in the office God has called us to and purposed us to be in. We also glorify

God best when we are working where He has ordained. Paul says, *Do All to the Glory of God.*

> **"All things are lawful," but not all things are helpful. "All things are lawful," but not all things build up.**
> **I Corinthians 10:23**

We should also be mindful of the fact that God will always provide confirmation of His call. The confirmation may come through another believer in whom you have confidence. It may come from signs and wonders that reveal His calling without any doubt, and sometimes (too often) it may come through the trials and tribulations associated with our attempts to avoid, deny, or run away from the call. Jonah comes to mind with the latter. Jonah 1:1 says,

> *Now the word of the* Lord *came to Jonah the son of Amit'tai, saying, "Arise, go to Nin'eveh, that great city, and cry against it; for their wickedness has come up before me."*

Now that is about as clear of an assignment from God as you can get. Straight to the point! Who was to go, where he was to go, and what he was to say. Jonah, however, had a different plan. Verse 3 says,

> *"But Jonah rose to flee to Tarshish from the presence of the* Lord.

> *He went down to Joppa and found a ship going to Tarshish; so he paid the fare, and went on board, to go with them to Tarshish, away from the presence of the Lord."*

You might recall that Jonah, for all intents and purposes, decided that Nineveh didn't deserve God's word or mercy, so he devised a different plan. That's Jonah's story, but each of us has our own. Although our stories vary, the motives are pretty much the same; we don't want to take on the assignment that God gives us, so we concoct a different strategy.

All of us that treaded in those waters have soon discovered that we can run from God, but we can't outrun God. In the end, after all of the dust settles (bellyaching, complaining, refusals, explanations, and reasons why we shouldn't do it), we realize that obedience is better than sacrifice. It's more comfortable too.

> *And Samuel said, "Hath the Lord as great delight in burnt offerings and sacrifices, as in obeying the voice of the Lord? Behold, to obey is better than sacrifice, and to hearken than the fat of rams." I Samuel 15:22*

Before you begin to think that I'm simplifying the process of accepting God's call, let me put a few things in perspective. First of all, the process is simple, but it isn't always easy. Secondly, I have heard countless stories from most preachers about how they tried to do anything but preach. Lastly, I need you to know that I am part of the second group.

I shared with you my story and experience as a toddler, when my parents later told me that encounter was when I was anointed to preach. Maybe if I had taken a different attitude and path as I grew up, things would have developed in a different manner. However, I didn't, and because of some regretful decisions I made along the way, I soon realized that there are consequences for our actions.

I John 1:9 assure us,

"If we confess our sins, God is faithful and just to forgive us our sins, and to cleanse us from all unrighteousness."

Every word in that passage is 100% true. What it doesn't say, however, is that although we are forgiven for whatever sin we commit, there will always be consequences for our actions.

When I was eighteen, I was living on my own, and although I wasn't living a wild and riotous life, I was having what I deemed "fun" in areas that obviously did not please God. I was still attending church. I often say that I was "in church," but the church wasn't really "in me." I didn't realize that we must continuously develop a relationship with God through the Holy Spirit.

One evening during the week, a friend asked me to attend a revival service at his church. I chose a night to go. The service was enjoyable, and the message was interesting. After the invitation was extended, the Elder stood up and started prophesying.

He would look over the congregation, point out someone, have him or her stand and then proceed to tell them what God had told him about their life. It started out kind of low-key but then began to intensify. People were crying, shouting, running around, and some were even screaming - "Praise the Lord."

Well, I had enough. I leaned over and told my friend, "I'm leaving. I'll see you tomorrow." I left, but I didn't realize that I would soon see that Elder again.

The next day, my friend called me to tell me he needed to talk with me. I met with him, thinking he probably wanted to apologize for my discomfort with the service. My church had lively services but not like that. When we met, he told me that after I left, the Elder said he was trying to get my attention because the Lord had given him a prophecy about my life. He asked my friend to give me his phone number to call him.

I said I would, but I avoided calling him for a week or two. For some reason (Holy Spirit), I couldn't seem to get that request off my mind. I finally decided to call him. What could a phone call hurt? I called; he answered and asked me if I would come by his house. He said he needed to discuss something with me. We set a date and time. We sat down, and he proceeded to tell me that "The Lord" told him that I was called to preach.

I listened to him for about 20 minutes. He explained that he would mentor, train, and prepare me for what I was called to do. He showed me books, talked about his journey in the ministry, and after he had said all that he thought was necessary, he asked me, *"so are you ready to get started?"*

I said, "no." He asked, why not? Do you have any questions? I said, "No, I don't." He said, "Then what is the reason for not accepting your call?" I said, "You said God told you that He called me to preach." He said, "Yes." I said, "Well, that's good, but if He wants me to preach, He is going to have to tell me, not you." He explained that God sometimes uses other people to convey calling – confirmation again.

I thanked him but stuck to my guns. You see, I was taught in my church that if God wants you to do something, he'll tell you. I decided that I would wait on Him to tell me. Yes, it is true that God will talk to you or communicate with or to you when He has an assignment for you, **but there must be clear lines for communication.**

Unconfessed sin and degenerate behavior impedes God's interaction with us. Maybe He had been trying to tell me that *now is the time* that He wanted me to preach.

Yes, my church had taught me that God will communicate

directly to us. What I didn't understand in that teaching was that I needed to be in a place where God could reach me.

Then the man and his wife heard the sound of the LORD God walking in the garden at the time of the evening breeze, and they hid themselves from the LORD God among the trees of the garden. ⁹ So the LORD God called out to the man and said to him, "Where are you?"

When God calls out to Adam and asks, "Where are you?" He's not searching for or looking for Adam. God is Sovereign and knows all things. He asks the question to see if Adam knew where he now was. Sin has a way of disconnecting you from God, causing doubt, fear, and distrust, all of which is unfounded but real. More likely than not, I would not have received a call from God, even if it was an audible one because I was living, distanced from God.

I wish I could tell you that like the prodigal, I came to myself, realized where I was, repented, and accepted God's call, but that was not what happened. I continued on the path that I established long enough to become less sensitive to the pulling of the Holy Spirit. I look back to that period of time and I see that God's mercy and grace were with me even though I in no way deserved it.

Later, I will explain how I became more aware of His presence and more willing to submit to His calling. I had to learn that while everyone experiences times of being physically alone, we don't have to be lonely. God is true to His word. He will never leave you!

"Haven't I commanded you: be strong and courageous? Do not be afraid or discouraged, for the L͟O͟R͟D͟ your God is with you wherever you go." Joshua 1:9

Chapter 4 - An Electrifying Experience

"And he said, Who art thou, Lord? And the Lord said I am Jesus whom you are persecuting: it is hard for you to kick against the pricks." Acts 9:5

It can be an interesting journey when your life has been set apart for the Lord's work, and you seem to do everything in opposition to it. I'm not suggesting that it is intentional defiance, but it is defiance nonetheless.

Even when we think we are doing the right things in life, just thinking they are right doesn't necessarily make them right. The right things done at the wrong time can still yield unpleasant results. In the eighth chapter of the book of Acts, we find the reporting of a vicious Saul who is going about critically persecuting Christians for what he believes is a good and worthy cause.

"And at that time there was a great persecution against the church which was at Jerusalem; and they were all scattered abroad throughout the regions of Judaea and Samaria, except the apostles. As for Saul, he made havoc of the church, entering into every house, and haling men and women committed them to prison." Acts 8:1b and 3.

It wasn't until God got his attention on Damascus road that he eventually began to see clearly that his actions were in opposition to God's will. We don't always understand it, but God allows some destructive things to go on for a while. However, when He says enough is enough, someone is about to experience the power of God. In this instance, Saul was about to have an electrifying experience.

In the next chapter, Acts 9:3-6, this day becomes Saul's reckoning day. The text says,

"And as he journeyed, he came near Damascus: and suddenly there shined round about him a light from heaven: And he fell to the earth, and heard a voice saying unto him, Saul, Saul, why are you persecuting me? And he said, Who art thou, Lord? And the Lord said I am Jesus whom you are persecuting: it is hard for you to kick against the pricks. And he trembling and astonished said, Lord, what wilt thou have me to do?"

When God gets our attention, there is no doubt in discerning it. Most will say as Saul did, *"what will you have me to do?"*

Every time God uses miracle power does not necessarily mean that He is attempting to get the attention of a wayward follower. Sometimes His faithful servants are tested, and while it may appear that they are outside of God's divine plan, they are not. They are just standing on His promises.

That's the situation we find the three Hebrew boys in. That does not in any way diminish God's powerful influence and involvement, however. They found themselves angering the King because of their commitment not to bow down to the King's image.

Even though they were not aware of what Jesus said in the Gospel of John, Chapter 16 and Verse 33, they were faithfully committed, even if it cost them their lives. If they could be this committed without knowing this passage, how much more should we be committed, having and knowing it?

"These things I have spoken unto you, that in me ye might have peace. In the world ye shall have tribulation: but be of good cheer; I have overcome the world."

These young men said ...

"If it be so, our God whom we serve is able to deliver us from the burning fiery furnace, and he will deliver us out of thine hand, O king." Daniel 3:17

This could have been an electrifying experience for them. Because God has a place of paradise prepared for us, He could have allowed the flames to burn their bodies, even to their death, and brought their souls into His bosom. In spite of what could be, they said,

"But if not, be it known unto thee, O king, that we will not

serve thy gods, nor worship the golden image which thou hast set up."

God didn't allow the fire to even put a smell in their clothing. Not only did He preserve them, this event caused the King to Bless God and as a result, scripture reflect these words,
Then Nebuchadnezzar spake, and said, "Blessed be the God of Shadrach, Meshach, and Abednego, who hath sent his angel, and delivered his servants that trusted in him, and have changed the king's word, and yielded their bodies, that they might not serve nor worship any god, except their own God."

When we take a stand for righteousness, we can't even comprehend the magnitude of what God is willing and able to do for us, and it is orchestrated by the power of the Holy Spirit. We are reminded of this at Ephesians 3:20.

"Now unto him that is able to do exceeding abundantly above all that we ask or think, according to the power that worketh in us,"

So, why do I point out these encounters? They remind me of a never-to-forget workday, years ago. My job was titled outside maintenance laborer. I had plans after work so I dressed up a bit.

My plan was to do as little as possible at work that day and just try to get through it as smoothly as possible. Wouldn't you know it, on this day we were given an assignment to break up concrete around a fire hydrant to repair a leaking valve.

I was content just standing around the job site watching the other guys take turns using a jackhammer. After watching for a while, I became a little fascinated with the power and ability of the jackhammer as it hammered through the concrete. One of the guys asked me if I wanted to try it out. Here again I thought, what could it hurt?

After operating it for a couple of minutes, I was intrigued. I didn't want to stop. I hammered and hammered until all of a sudden everything just went silent. It was almost as if time stood still. I began to feel intense heat and a burning sensation, but I kept squeezing the handle, and the hammer kept digging in until everything just stopped, hammer and all.

I stepped back, looked around and everybody that had been working with me were about 50-75 feet away. They slowly came toward me and assisted in getting the jackhammer out of my hands, and explaining to me that I had been hammering into an underground powerline for about 10 minutes. Fire was spewing out of the hole I had created with the jackhammer, yet I was continuously squeezing the trigger, I had gone into shock.

My clothing was about 50% burned, and the other 50%

melted. My leather jacket was like burned charcoal; it just crumbled at the touch. The crew said they ran a distance away to protect themselves. They thought I was dead!

I was taken to the medical department and later to the hospital. No one could explain it, but I had only suffered second and third-degree burns to half of my face. My right eye suffered flash-burn, but there was no vision loss. The power line that I hammered into was forty-eight hundred volts. I hammered through a power line that shutdown 4 maintenance and production buildings. All I could hear was, "there's no way anyone could have survived this." Yet, here I was, alive and all things considered, very minimally injured.

The hospital sent me home, and it was projected that I would probably be off work for about 3-4 months. It was as if someone had divided my face vertically in half. One side was brown and the other side was pink. The doctors provided ointment and pain meds but would not say if my pigmentation would ever return to normal.

Six weeks later, I reported back to work with no evidence of the accident ever occurring. Vast numbers of employees came to me and said they could not believe the healing. Some said it was unexplainable. So many said I was really lucky. I appreciated all of their comments, love, concern, and explanations, but I came to realize it was only God. When the Bible says that God is Jehovah

Raphe, *the God who heals*, that's what He does.

I am no better than anyone else that has been burned, and I have the scars to prove it. I am just one of God's children that He decided to provide the level of Grace that yielded the results of no scarring. Furthermore, whenever things turn out this way, it's for His glory, not mine; Nothing more, nothing less. I, without a doubt, deserved much less, but He provided much more. What a mighty God we serve!

When Jesus heard it, He said, "This sickness will not end in death but is for the glory of God, so that the Son of God may be glorified through it." John 11:4

Chapter 5 – The Drum & the Real Estate Deal

"Look, does it make sense to truly become successful, but then to hand over your very soul? What is your soul really worth?"
Matthew 16:26

Being a disciple of Christ is much like being an apprentice. In fact, discipleship is defined as a follower, a learner, or one who patterns his life after his teacher. I can relate to these definitions because I experienced apprenticeship training. Whether discipleship or apprenticeship, it is a training program that involves continuous training. Mastering it does not happen overnight. It requires exposure to various situations and building a toolbox of tools or spiritual tools to properly address each scenario.

Then Jesus spoke to them again: "I am the light of the world. Anyone who follows Me, will never walk in the darkness but will have the light of life." John 8:12

Discipleship/Apprenticeship is a journey towards becoming. Maybe that's why upon completion, you earn the right to be called a "Journeyman." In my apprenticeship, I rotated every six months to a new area, a new shift, or a new Journeyman. Sometimes all three changed.

The purpose was simply to expose each apprentice to different personalities, aspects of maintenance environments, varying skill-sets, and techniques that could be used to resolve and maintain equipment. Each technique required certain tools to properly address the problem.

I encountered some interesting Journeymen during my 4 years of apprenticing. Some were very knowledgeable and willing to pour into the apprentices. There were others that seemed to be anticipating the end of the 6 months as much as we were. Either way, when it was time to rotate to a new area, we were assessed and evaluated to track our learning, growth, and development.

When Jesus was going about choosing his disciples or we could say apprentices, He simply said to them, "Follow Me." His assessment was both intuitive and through observation. Many of these men were fisherman, so it makes sense that He said to them,

"Follow Me," He told them, "and I will make you to become a fisher for people!" Matthew 4:19

It's a process of becoming, and the greatest teacher ever, Jesus Christ, simply says, "Follow Me!" It is amazing sometimes what you can pick up by simply following someone, good or bad. Whom we follow can expose us to some very valuable traits, but the result is not totally predicated on just following but how we perceive the things we experience while following.

We have one example of this precept with the disciples Jesus chose. Although each one of the disciples had their own unique personality, their motives were unique as well. On one occasion, a request for a special position was made by the mother of James and John.

"As Jesus was speaking about the things that were to come, Zebedee's wife, whose sons were among Jesus' disciples, came to Jesus with her sons and knelt down before Him to ask a favor. Jesus asked, what do you want? She said, When the kingdom of God is made manifest, I want one of my boys, James and John, to sit at Your right hand, and one to sit at Your left hand."

Matthew 20:20-21

While this request did not come directly from James or John, they were with her so we might conclude that they were not in opposition to it. When apprenticing, it can become hazardous and even dangerous when the apprentice is not focused on the right things. Many have been cut, injured, and in some instances lost fingers, etc. because they were focused on some part of the work but not on the entire process.

Jesus told the mother of James and John, *"You don't know what you are asking for. Are ye able to drink of the cup that I shall drink of, but to sit on my right hand, and on my left, is not mine to give, but it shall be given to them for whom it is prepared of my*

Father." Maybe this is where James and John's mind was. They had seen Jesus perform so many miracles and the attention He received because of it.

It can become easy to slip into a spirit of pride if you're not careful. One thing I learned quickly as an apprentice is that everything looks easier when the Journeyman is doing it, but how quickly things change when I was told to do it.

In a training session many years ago I learned something that I never forgot. I used that concept later when I was a journeyman teaching apprentices. The method was, tell them what you are about to do, demonstrate it by doing it, coach them as they do it, and then have them do it themselves. I apply that concept in my daily life with other assignments.

"They had come down from the mountain, and as they headed toward town, they came to a crowd. As they approached the crowd, a man rushed up to Jesus and knelt before Him. Lord, have mercy on my son. He has seizures. Sometimes when they come on, my son falls into the fire or into a pond. We are very concerned for him. <u>I brought him to Your disciples, but they could not heal him</u>."
Matthew 17:14-15

It can be embarrassing when you get involved with a job or responsibility or a ministry, and you discover while engaged that you didn't get all of the details. Sometimes, you don't get a second chance to recover from a failed attempt.

Jesus healed the man's son. Later, while alone, the disciples asked Jesus why they could not heal the boy. Jesus shared some valuable information with them that is valuable for us as well. He said,

"If you have faith as a grain of a mustard seed, you will tell this mountain, 'Move from here to there,' and it will move. Nothing will be impossible for you. However, this kind does not come out except by prayer and fasting." Matthew 17:20-21

Being successful in our ministries is not based solely on how we do what we do. It is more predicated on being connected to the power source, the Great Healer. Some problems or illnesses are like demons. They latch on and won't seem to let go. If it is God's will that a circumstance changes or a person is healed, then great faith, prayer, and fasting are often required. The disciples had to learn this, and so do we.

During my first two rotations in my apprenticeship, I had some of the best Journeymen that any apprentice could dream of. They were knowledgeable, patient, and considerate. It's been 45 years and I still remember them: Ed Byers, Bill Lockwood, Pat Shelton, Paul Kesler, Paul Ramerez, and a guy everyone called three-finger Mike (for obvious reason).

These guys, in their own unique way, taught me to watch,

observe, think things over, and ask questions. They would say – *"Better to measure twice and cut once."* That was valuable advice. I didn't realize how valuable until I rotated to other Journeymen that did not have the same affinity toward apprentices. I was not the only one to have these experiences. Yes, there were apprentices of different ethnicities, genders, and age groups. Many of them encountered at one time or another, a Journeyman that just didn't seem to be intrigued having an apprentice assigned to them.

A couple of years later, I was part of a small crew on an afternoon shift that finished jobs that were unfinished from dayshift. I often applied the concepts of *"watch, observe, think things over, and ask questions* with these jobs because we didn't see how the work was done on the other shift.

One day we were given an assignment of putting in a sump pump crock. If you don't know what a crock is, it is the round cylinder structure below a street drain cover. As we attempted to dig the dirt out to put in the crock, the dirt around the hole began to cave in. After several attempts to hold the dirt back, one of the journeymen suggested that we use a metal drum instead.

The plan was to remove the drum lid by cutting around the drum with a cutting torch. When I inspected the metal drum, I smelled something unusual inside of it. I suggested taking it outside and washing it out. The journeyman told me, "Ah, it'll be okay." I thought about what I had learned years ago (watch, observe, think things over, and ask questions) and decided to stand away from the drum as he was cutting. As soon as the flame from the torch penetrated the drum, it exploded!

From my peripheral, I saw Joe being lifted into the air. I crawled out of the pit from the other end, and when I came back to the worksite, Joe was lying on the floor and his coveralls were burning. By this time, the other apprentice showed up, and we mustered up enough courage to go in and shut the oxygen and propane tanks down. We grabbed an extinguisher and put out the flames on Joe.

With all of the adrenalin flowing, I didn't realize that I had hurt my knee and back. We both were taken to the hospital. Joe had broken his ankle, fractured his hip, and sustained minor burns. He was placed on medical leave for about 4 months. Although painful, my injuries were not serious. I was treated and was back to work a couple of days later. When I thought about what happened and what could have happened, again, God protected me from a situation that could have been much worse. I still didn't sense Him trying to get my attention.

I was a part-time real estate agent during this time. While I was off, I was setting up appointments to show houses. On the morning of the day I was to return to work, I was planning to show a house before going to work. I was going to be early for my appointment so I changed my plans.

I knew that our office had another listing that was similar to the house I was going to show, so I called the office for the lockbox code. I thought, I'll go by and take a look at the other house. If they don't like the one I show them, I can show them this one.

I knocked on the door and no one was home, so I used the code and went in. I walked through a few rooms and when I entered the dining room, there was a bear rug on the floor. I wondered if it was a real bear until I saw a gun case full of rifles. I got kind of nervous. I thought, I'll take a look at the basement and then leave for my appointment. When I got to the basement door, I had a strange feeling in my gut and decided not to go down there.

As soon as I stepped one foot on the porch, a guy on a motorcycle rode up. He was yelling at me, even before he stopped. "Don't You Move!" I had no idea what was going on, but I decided to step completely outside of the house. He began to press me about being in his house. I told him I was a real estate agent and I could show him my card. He took the card and called our office.

After the office provided confirmation, he told me there had been burglaries in the neighborhood and that he was a federal officer. He explained that he had a *do not show* clause with his listing without prior approval. He opened his jacket and showed me a pistol and said if he had arrived while I was in the house, I would have been dead.

We cleared things up, and in the end had a calm

conversation. He said, in the future, have the office call me when you want to show my house. I said no worries. I will never show this house. When I left, I went to my appointment, showed that house and headed to work. I told the guys at work what happened. They could see I had some kind of week. I may not have sensed God's presence, but I do know that,

"God is our protection and source of strength. He is always ready to help us in times of trouble. So we are not afraid when the earth quakes and the mountains fall into the sea. We are not afraid when the seas become rough and dark and the mountains tremble." Psalms 46:1-4

Chapter 6 – A Quiet Place

"He makes me lie down in green pastures. He leads me beside peaceful waters. He renews my soul. He guides me along the paths of righteousness for the sake of his name."

Psalms 23:2-3

When I look back at the countless times I sort of snubbed God, I get kind of nervous. He caused, allowed, and permitted so many things to happen in my life, but I just didn't get it. Maybe I just wouldn't accept it? Psalms 46 begins with a reminder that God is our sanctuary and strength. It ends at Verse 11 with an attention-getting announcement,

"Be still, and know that I am God.
I am exalted among the nations.
I am exalted in the earth."

It's not like I hadn't been exposed to the ways of God. I should have known it was Him speaking. Isaiah 40:20-21 says,
"Don't you know, haven't you heard or even been told from your earliest memories how the earth came to be. Who else could have done it except God, enthroned high above the earth? From such a vantage point, people seem like grasshoppers to Him. Who else

but God could stretch out the skies as if they were a curtain, draw them tight, and suspend them over our heads like the roof of a tent?"

Who else but a loving, compassionate God could and would provide unmerited protection to a hard-headed person like me? I don't know if I was rebelling against God or my obstinate behavior prevented Him from getting my attention. I do know that wayward living can impede our inability to hear or sense His beckoning. I discovered the answer when I was in a quiet place. God revealed to me that *"there was too much noise in my life."* That is so true for so many.

In I Samuel, we read about Hannah and how much she desired to have a child. She made a commitment to God that if He gave her a child, she would in turn give him back to the Lord. God blessed Hannah with a son and she kept her vow. After reaching the proper age, she sent Samuel to live with Eli the Priest. When God decided it was time to call Samuel into ministry, Samuel did not recognize or understand that it was God speaking to him. He thought it was Eli that was speaking to him.

At I Samuel 3:9-10, we read Eli's instructions to Samuel. ***He told Samuel, "Go and lie down. If He calls you, say, 'Speak, Lord, for Your servant is listening.'" So Samuel went and lay down in his place. The Lord came, stood there, and called as before,***

> *"Samuel, Samuel!" Samuel responded, "Speak, for Your servant is listening."*

Sometimes, inexperience, immaturity, or just too much noise can interfere with our understanding and ability to discern God's voice. After being instructed what to do, Samuel is now positioned to receive what God has for him. He properly responded, "Speak Lord for your servant is listening." That's what our response should be when we are being called into ministry.

Unfortunately, that's not what usually happens. I had too much noise in my life, and I tried all sorts of alternatives to find meaning in what I was experiencing. As a young man with exceptional income and excessive material possessions, ministry was the last thing I wanted in my life. God however, was saying, "Now Is The Time."

> *"We plan the way we want to live, but only GOD makes us able to live it." Proverbs 16:9*

I found myself becoming very irritated and uncomfortable with things that used to provide excitement and contentment. It seemed like whatever I was doing or wherever I was, my mind was overcome with a pulling in another direction. I decided to seek advice from my assistant pastor, but I didn't want him to know my questions were about me.

I started attending his Sunday morning class where I thought I could disguise my questions and no one would figure out that I was searching for my own answers. I remember asking my first question: *how does a person find out what God wants them to do?* His answer was simple. He said you just go to God in prayer and ask Him. I thought wow, that's easy enough, so I did, but I didn't get an answer.

The next week I told him that "the guy" did what he said and still didn't get an answer. He then added, well, the prayer must be earnest and sincere. I thought to myself, I think I was sincere. I said okay, I'll tell him. I spent all week in what I thought was earnest and sincere prayer but still, no message from God.

While I was heeding all of the advice he was giving me, I was still experiencing the same discomfort in the Sunday morning preaching services. It just seemed like the pastor was preaching to me. No matter what the subject was, all I was hearing was: *When God is calling you to ministry, the best thing you can do is submit unto His authority, accept His appointment and get busy.* Now I was getting frustrated and angry. I decided to start attending other church services. I didn't want to hear what I was hearing.

I tried three different churches, but the results were the same. It just seemed like the message being preached was specifically being preached to me. All I heard was - *When God is calling you to ministry, the best thing you can do is submit unto His authority, accept His appointment and get busy.* The next Sunday, I decided to go back to my church. I thought to myself, if I'm going to hear the same message, I might as well be at my own church.

I remember this Sunday because it was Mother's Day. I went to the Sunday morning class and the assistant pastor asked me how the guy was doing that I had been asking questions about. I told him that he said he still hasn't got an answer from God. He said he didn't understand that, then paused and said, "you know the only thing I can think of that could be a problem is *"unconfessed sin."* When he said that, it hit me like a ton of bricks. While my prayers may have been earnest and sincere, they were not pure because my behavior was full of reproach. I became nervous and shaky because of my audacity. I instantly thought of I John 1:9,

"But if we own up to our sins, God shows that He is faithful and just by forgiving us of our sins and purifying us from the pollution of all the bad things we have done."

I asked for God's forgiveness and got prepared for the worship service. I went in, took my seat, and all seemed to be going well. I felt better and was not irritated or uncomfortable. I was thinking to myself, He's going to speak to me tonight and tell me what He wants me to do.

As the service moved along, everything was going quite smoothly. There were a couple of Mother's Day tributes and songs from the choir, and then the pastor approached the podium to speak. About halfway through his message, I began to feel that discomfort I had been getting before. This time, however, it was aggressive. I said to myself, when the invitation to discipleship is offered, I'm going to leave and go downstairs.

The invitation was extended and I got up to leave. Somehow, almost like transcendence, I found myself walking toward the front of the church instead of toward the rear doors. I didn't realize where I was until I had reached the front of the church. I just stood there. People were strangely looking at me; at least I thought they were. I was trying to figure out how I got there.

One of the Deacons came over and asked me why I came forward. I told him I needed to talk to the pastor. The pastor took me into his office, and I told him, "I have been called to preach." He said I have been waiting on you to acknowledge this. Do you want to go before the church and tell them? I said yes, and he led me back and announced to the church that I had something I wanted to say.

I stood there as he spoke and planned my words carefully. I wanted this moment to be a great one. Before I could say a word, I broke down in tears; the church erupted into tears, praise, hallelujahs. All I could say was – "God has called me to preach, and I am accepting His call." So many people came to me after service and revealed that they had been shown this already; they were just waiting on me to confess it.

"But you, Timothy, man of God: Run for your life from all this. Pursue a righteous life—a life of wonder, faith, love, steadiness, courtesy. Run hard and fast in the faith. Seize the eternal life, the life you were called to, the life you so fervently embraced in the presence of so many witnesses." I Timothy 6:12

It's not that I believed my calling was sure, based on these witnesses; they just provided additional assurance. I had now finally surrendered to the sovereign God that was patiently nudging me and compassionately waiting for me to acknowledge and accept His call. Now I needed someone mature in the ministry to walk me through the process of development.

One of my blood brothers was in the ministry and had been for a number of years. I consulted with him and he told me the best thing I could do was enroll in Detroit Bible College where he was attending; so, I did. It was there that I was introduced to Dean S. J. Williams. Dr. Williams was in his 80s and full of both Bible knowledge and wisdom. I was amazed at how he simplified the path to become a competent minister of the gospel.

I remember so many simple statements that Dean Williams used to convey salient points. He would explain why it was important for ministers to study. He referred to II Timothy 2:15,

Study to show yourself approved unto God, a workman that needeth not to be ashamed, rightly dividing the word of truth.

He would follow that instruction with, *"So many preachers preach junky messages because they are full of junk, instead of the word."*

Sometimes in classes where all of the students were preachers, conversations would come up about being called to preach. A lot of the preachers in those classes came across as though the call alone qualified them to preach. When Dean Williams overheard those kinds of conversations, he would say, *"You were called in <u>preparation</u> to preach."*

He would remind us that the call doesn't prepare the preacher; the relationship with Jesus Christ does. He would also explain to us that we are not preaching our gospel; it is the Gospel of Jesus Christ. So, get to know Him and your message will have power.

Dean Williams had a passion for preachers. He was also highly respected and recognized among his peers. I recall several occasions where a church needed a pastor and their pulpit committee would contact Dean Williams and ask whom he might recommend. I remember so many fellow ministers in class that were recommended and accepted as pastors when I attended Detroit Bible College. Who knows, some of them may still be.

Dean used to say to those pastoring or pursuing pastoring: "If you love your sheep, they will stand up for you, even when you're wrong, but if you mistreat them, they won't stand with you, even when you're right. His message was a message conveying the importance of loving those that God has placed in your care.

He used to tell those of us that were married to make sure we maintained a loving environment in our home. He would explain, as a pastor, you are going to encounter struggles and challenges with your congregation, with your fellow pastors and ministers, on your jobs, if you are a bi-vocational pastor, and even when you are out and about. He would say that these are some of the ways in which Satan uses others to wear you down and weaken your ability to do the work of the ministry. However, if you can keep your home a safe haven, you can make it. Even when these other entities beat you down, if you can just get home, although you might have to fall in the door, a loving wife and family can provide the love and motivation to go on.

There is so much that I could say about the impact Dean Williams had on me and my ministry, but I will stop with this. He constantly reminded us that God had called us to a work that is just that, WORK! He said most of the time, it is a struggle. However, he reminded us: "struggles will strengthen you if you don't allow them to crush you."

I have been in ministry for many years now and have found all of his advice to be both true and helpful. I'm reminded of one salient point he made that I hold on to more than anything else. He said we must consistently set aside quality time to spend with God in prayer and meditation. It is in those times that He will speak to and minister to us. In that quiet place I saturate myself with the words found at Psalms 62:8.

"Trust in him at all times; ye people, pour out your heart before him: God is a refuge for us."

Chapter 7 - Make You To Become

"God's law is perfect, turning lives around. His words are reliable and true, instilling wisdom to open minds." Psalm 19:7

In Chapter 4, I referenced Matthew 4:19 where Jesus said to His potential disciples, "Follow Me and I will make you fishers of men." The amplified version says it this way,

"Follow Me as My disciples, accepting Me as your Master and Teacher and walking the same path of life that I walk, and I will make you fishers of men."

One thing I've learned on this journey is that there are no short cuts in ministry development. You must put in the time. I have been given all kinds of advice in terms of what I needed to do to grow. Some told me that I needed to read the whole Bible 3 or four times. Others said that I needed to preach every time I had an opportunity and that practice would develop my growth. Several schools were recommended. I was even told to move from my current church and learn under the leadership of other pastors and other churches.

While I will agree that all of those suggestions have benefits, they alone would not necessarily accomplish the growth and development that I needed for my specific call. The message of the gospel is the same, and it never changes. The method, however, does. God created each one of us in His own unique way, and the same is true for ministers. He does not change our personalities. After all, He knows who we really are. God uses the unique qualities that He infused into us by transforming our minds as we spend time with Him. Then, at the right time (and He determines when that is), He guides us and equips us to do the special work that He has assigned to us.

That's why we can't and shouldn't pattern our ministry after someone else. Allow me to use an illustration from my apprenticeship. There were about 24 apprentices that started their apprenticeship about the same time as I did. We all finished within 6 to 9 months of each other. We had to put in a certain number of work hours (about 8200) and complete 17 classes. If you put in extra hours and took a heavy course load, you could finish sooner.

Once completed, each one of us was called a journeyman. Our journeyman status varied. Some were journeymen electricians, journeyman pipefitters, journeymen carpenters, journeymen millwrights, etc. Now, if a journeymen electrician patterned his work practices after a journeymen pipefitter, his career would not last very long. Each journeyman had specific skills, and collectively, the necessary equipment would be maintained and repaired. No one was more important than the other. No one journeyman was expected to maintain all aspects of the equipment, but together, every aspect of the equipment was kept in working order.

The same is true in ministry. Every community is different and therefore has different needs. Every church has its own unique makeup. While every church needs Jesus and the message of the gospel, how it is administered varies from church to church. The church and all of its members belong to God. Therefore, God calls and/or sends the person that He deems the right fit into each church body to lead that congregation into fulfilling the calling He has placed on that body of believers.

That's why it is incumbent upon us to seek His guidance and direction when we either set out to find a pastor or desire to become a pastor. (Nothing could be more uncomfortable than being in a place that God has not called you to). It is not uncommon to find some churches struggling because they chose a pastor that God did not choose for that church. That doesn't mean that they are not being productive, or the gospel is not being preached. It just means that there is a lot of unnecessary struggle because they are functioning more under the permissive will of God and not His divine will.

I'm not going to dive too deep into the variations of God's will, but I will say this: God will sometimes exercise His sovereign will, He will sometimes utilize His perceptive will, and then there are times when He will allow His permissive will.

- *When God said, "Let there be light," He issued a divine imperative. He exercised His **sovereign will.** It was impossible for the light not to appear.*
- *The **perceptive will** of God relates to the revealed commandments of God's published law. Where it was not possible for the light to refuse to shine in creation, it is possible for us to refuse to obey this command.*
- *The distinction between the sovereign will of God and the **permissive will** of God tends to generate untold confusion. What is usually meant by divine permission is that God simply lets it happen. That is, He does not directly intervene to prevent its happening.*

Regardless of our choice, in the end, God's will, will be done, and He will get the glory. What varies, however, are the consequences we experience. It is always better and less traumatic when we consult Him first and align our will with His.

So much of what we learn in life comes about through experiences. Paul reminds us at Galatians 5:16,

"But I say, walk habitually in the Holy Spirit, seek Him and be responsive to His guidance, and then you will certainly not carry out the desire of the sinful nature which responds impulsively without regard for God and His precepts."

This transformation does not come about overnight; the process is progressive. When our heart's desire is to please Him, we become more sensitive to His voice, His leading, and His will as we seek to make decisions in life. As we grow, develop, and mature, we initiate that process of becoming who He has called us to be.

Someone said to me years ago - "*Show me your friends, and I'll show you your future.*" That sounded plausible and a bit sophisticated, so I thought it might be true. Later, I discovered that those words came from the Wisdom of Solomon. Proverbs 13:20 says,

"He that walketh with wise men shall be wise: but a companion of fools shall be destroyed."

Being with someone physically will not necessarily morph you into being that individual or even being like them. What it does do, however, is stir up a sense of comfort or discomfort within our spirits. Being with wise people that are moving productively forward usually produces a calming within our spirit, and a yearning to be around them because of it. That calming is often the Holy Spirit confirming the relationship.

When we are in the company of unwise or as the Bible refers to them, foolish people, a believer's heart should at some point sense discomfort or uneasiness. This is most often the Holy Spirit alerting us that this relationship is headed for destruction. Proverbs

27:12 warns us,

> *"Wise people will see trouble coming and avoid it, but an unthinking person will walk right into it and regret it later."*

I often pray, Lord, help me to see trouble coming, long before it gets here, and give me the *wisdom* to know what to do and the *courage* to do it.

The Christian walk is just as much a process of becoming as birth is to adulthood. Every encounter in life provides an opportunity to grow, freeze, or retreat. There will be times when any one of the three is appropriate, but a continuous embrace of either of these can restrict your process of becoming. Growing is very productive, but it must be monitored. A total focus on personal growth can cause one to become insensitive, cold, and perhaps even callused when dealing with other believers that may not have reached to your level of maturity.

Growth, for believers, occurs threefold: upward, outward, and downward. We grow upward in our relationship with God, outward in our relationship with people around us (Christians and Non-Christians), and downward as we acquire roots while developing our foundation in the word. When orchestrated properly, we become rock-solid in our walk. If out of sync, we get things out of order, and our walk, our witness, and our testimony can become problematic. It's a balancing act. We must never forget that people see us long before they hear us.

So, just as Jesus called his disciples with the message, "Follow Me, and I will make you to become Fishers of Men," He calls each one of us with the same message. Our journey may be different and our labor fields may vary, but His message remains the same. Every call from Jesus is a call to Jesus. It also includes a call to leave some things behind. In that, we must trust Him. Luke put it this way,

"So they pulled their boats up on shore, left everything and followed Him." Luke 5:11.

Chapter 8 – A Balancing Act

"A person's soul is the Lord's lamp. It searches his entire innermost being." Proverbs 20:27

Balance is so vitally important in every aspect of our life. It is balance that enables a child to move from crawling to walking. It can be a funny spectacle when you observe the beginning stages and attempts of a toddler mustering up the courage to embark upon the liberation of walking. They will spread their arms out, probably not realizing that their arms provide the means for them to balance their body as they take each step. After a number of practice runs, they eventually walk around without using their arms for balance; the necessary muscles have developed and they walk almost effortlessly now.

I remember the early days of my apprenticeship. Occupational Safety & Health Administration (OSHA) guidelines were not as stringent as they are today. When we worked overhead on jobs, such as hanging bridges, reinforcing trusts, hanging conveyor track and other like jobs, we occasionally took serious risks. Perhaps there were OSHA restrictions and we chose not to follow them. Not out of defiance, we just figured we could successfully navigate the risk. Most of the time we were successful or dodged the bullet, so to speak, but every now and again, injuries did occur. Thank God they were usually minor.

One part of those jobs that always troubled me was walking out to the center of a beam to unhitch the strap from the crane's hook. I watched journeymen do it all the time, but I just feared losing my balance and falling to the floor (sometimes 20-30 feet below). So my method of removing the strap involved crawling out on my hands and knees or sliding out on my butt. It got the job done, but it was nowhere near as brave or daring as walking out. As I moved along in my apprenticeship, I eventually developed the courage and balance to walk the beams, almost effortlessly.

That's about the time when most people have accidents. We continue to do things that we know are not correct, legal or God's way of doing them but we keep getting away with it. The more we get away with it, without noticeable damage, the more we continue to do it. Not only do we continue to do it, but we also show less regard for the risk associated with it.

I reached a place where I almost welcomed the opportunities to walk the beam. If an apprentice or an audience was nearby, that was all the better.

Apostle Paul warns us about getting too arrogant or overconfident in Verse 3 of Romans Chapter 12. He says,

"Because of the grace allotted to me, I can respectfully tell you not to think of yourselves as being more important than you are;

devote your minds to sound judgment since God has assigned to each of us a measure of faith."

Paul urges all of us who read his letters in the Word of God to respond by offering our bodies (eyes, ears, feet, hands, and mouths) to God as a living sacrifice to Him. Paul is not suggesting that we offer the kind of sacrifice that ends in death. He is reminding us that the sacrifice of our Lord, Jesus Christ, changed everything. His resurrection from the grave stole life from death and makes it possible for those who trust in Him to become a sacrifice, and yet live.

What does that kind of living look like? First of all, we put an end to living with a focus on the patterns of this world. Once that commitment is made, with the help of the Holy Spirit, we begin to live in constant renewal by the transformation of our minds: the way we think, act, feel, speak, and touch those around us. We simply begin to process the world around us in a manner consistent with the will and purposes of God.

In fairness, I must admit that Paul had some advantages. He did not have the responsibilities of marriage, caring for children, aging parents, or a job that demanded onerous hours. Most of us have some of those challenges, but there was a time when we didn't. How committed were we then? Speaking for myself, I know I could have done more during those years when there was less demand.

God expects impartiality, objectivity, and integrity in our Christian walk. The most easygoing way to accomplish this is by invoking balance in our lives. You probably know people that can't seem to get anything completed, in spite of the time allotted them. They will tell you that time just seemed to fly by. On the other hand, there are people that maximize their time, and it seems like God gives them more than 24 hours in their day. The answer is simple; it's a balancing act.

At Exodus 20:3, God commands, **"You are not to serve any other gods before Me."** This is both simple and right to the point. Not that He needed to, but God could have reminded Israel of all the victories He provided over every opposing enemy, but He didn't. You would think that would have been realized. Nevertheless, at II Kings 17:37, they are instructed again, **"Be careful to observe all the laws, statutes, ordinances, and commands I have inscribed for you. And do not revere or worship any other gods."**

"If any widow has children or grandchildren, then go to the descendants first and teach them that it is their spiritual responsibility to care for their own family,to repay their parents and grandparents because this is what pleases God."
I Timothy 5:4

We are admonished not to give any idol thing or person first place or priority in our lives. We are reminded that the responsibility of taking care of our families is also an expectation of God. Maintaining proper order in accomplishing this requires the preserving of balance in our lives. We are also counseled at I Timothy 3:5,

"If someone can't manage his own household, then how can he take care of God's family?"

We should not ignore either, and one does not dominate the other. There must be a balance in place, or there will ultimately become problems. There are no super Christians and there are no super parents. Everything that God entrusts to us is expected to be governed by the Word of God but not to an extreme that causes one of those responsibilities to be overlooked or abandoned.

Proper balance is established when we begin our planning and decision-making in devotion and meditation with God. This prepares our heart and minds to receive Godly guidance and direction for the day. The plans and decisions that will impact our families should filter through that amalgamation. The stress that often accompanies decision-making can be greatly reduced when we know that, in spite of the discomfort, it is yet God's will.

"We ought to obey God rather than men."
Acts 5:29b
"Seek first the kingdom of God and His righteousness, and all

> *these things will be provided for you."*
> *Matthew 6:33*
>
> *"Acknowledge Him in all your ways and He will direct your paths."*
> *Proverbs 3:6*

When we fail to begin with God, we usually end up with unsettling situations and circumstances.

Because our journey on this side is progressive, we will occasionally experience discomfort, even when we consult God for direction. At times, God has us on a growth mission, and the struggles and discomfort become the vehicles used to keep us close to Him.

> *"I take pleasure in infirmities, in reproaches, in necessities, in persecutions, in distresses for Christ's sake: for when I am weak, then am I strong." II Corinthians 12:10*

I can, however, say in all sincerity that every time I chose to make critical decisions and did not consult God first, it wasn't long before I found myself in hot water. Remembering the faithfulness of God and the countless times He has forgiven, restored and re-established me, ushered me back into balance with Him.

Steve Jevans points out in a study conducted in 2011 how the children of Israel in the wilderness provides an example of a people that were in desperate need of balance. Four hundred years of tangible oppression in Egypt should have been no comparison to the challenges they experienced on their wilderness journey, but oh, did it ever. Those ten encounters are listed below.

1. *Exodus14:10-14 - Pharaoh and the Egyptian army was behind Israel. They complain against Moses. Said it was better to serve in Egypt than die in wilderness. Moses promises them that God will fight for them, and they should be quiet. God Blocked the Egyptians with a cloud, divided the Red Sea and destroyed the Egyptians as they chased.*

2. *Exodus15:23-27 - At Marah, the bitterness where they could not drink water. They murmured against Moses and said, what shall we drink? Moses cried to Lord and he was showed a tree which made the waters sweet. They were told that if they would listen to God none of the diseases of the Egyptians would affect them.*

3. *Exodus16:1-14 - Wilderness of Sin with no food. They murmured against Moses and said, would to God we had died when we sat by the flesh pots in Egypt. You brought us out here to die of hunger. The Lord addresses them, Moses relays the message. God provides manna, and quail daily.*

4. *Exodus16:19-21 - Wilderness of sin in gathering the manna. Disobedience of Moses' command to leave none until morning. Moses was wroth. He burst in rage. It bred worms, stank and melted.*

5. *Exodus16:22-30 - Wilderness of sin, again in gathering manna. Disobedience of Moses' command not to gather on Sabbath. The Lord rebukes him, then as commanded he gathers a portion for a memorial in the Ark. God asks Moses, how long will you refuse to keep my commandments and my laws?*

6. *Exodus17:1-7 - At Rephidim there was no water and he was chided. They Contended with Moses, asking for water, questioning whether the Lord was amongst them or not. They asked why they were brought out of Egypt to be killed. They cried out to the Lord. The people were almost ready to stone him. God commands Moses to spite the rock before the elders. The Lord stands on the rock and water flows out when smitten.*

7. *Exodus 32:1-34:35 - At Sinai, Moses was on the Mount for 40 days and they fell into Idolatry. Aaron makes the golden calf and they have a feast day. Moses reminded the Lord of*

covenant He made with Abraham. He broke the Tablets of law. He would have destroyed the people or left them to an angel to lead into land. Instead, He turned His wrath based on intercession and showed glory with a renewed and modified covenant.

8. Numbers11:1-3 - They were three days from Mt Sinai; Taberah. The People complained. Moses said nothing but Lord God addressed them directly. They cried out to Moses and although he prayed and stopped fire, God sent fire which burnt amongst them and consumed those on the outside of the camp.

9. Numbers11:4-35 - Kibroth-hattaavah, translated (Graves of Lust) because the people lusted after food other than manna. Moses cries out to the Lord that the burden is too great. Doubts what Lord will do. Lord puts spirit upon the 70; sends 3 feet deep of quail and while they eat (months' worth), as they ate God sent great plague killing many.

10. Numbers13:25-14:39 - In the Wilderness of Paran, at border of Canaan, they murmured against Moses believing that they could not conquer. Begin to make captain to return to Egypt, question why wives and children should be destroyed.

Seek to stone Joshua and Caleb Fell on face in prayer. Pleads for glory of name of Lord despite people's great sin. God at first will destroy, but He pardons according to Moses' intercession. Promises that they will wander for 40 years. All spies except Joshua and Caleb died immediately.

Most students of the Bible have read or heard about the ten plagues that God used to persuade Pharaoh to release the Israelites from enslavement in Egypt. Their lack of faith, their inability to remember where God had brought them from, and their loss of focus, created the perfect recipe for imbalance. God said at Numbers 4:22 – 24,

"Because all those men which have seen my glory, and my miracles, which I did in Egypt and in the wilderness, and have tempted me now these ten times, and have not hearkened to my voice; Surely they shall not see the land which I sware unto their fathers, neither shall any of them that provoked me see it: But my servant Caleb, because he had another spirit with him, and hath followed me fully, him will I bring into the land where he went; and his seed shall possess it."

As followers of Christ process all of this, it should not be difficult to grasp. I can only speak for myself, but I have well surpassed 10 occasions in my life of testing God by complaining about my circumstances. God has parted waters in my life and has turned many bitter situations into sweet ones. God has bestowed so much undeserving mercy and grace toward me. I have missed out on so many opportunities because of my disobedience and hard-headedness. No matter what we call it, it is plainly, and simply, sin.

So, at the end of the day, I'm no better than the Israelites. I doubt that I stand alone in that regard. Whether you seem to have a good handle in your walk or you are failing miserably, our success in this endeavor weighs heavily on focusing on balance. God does not desire to withhold anything from us. He wants us to keep things in perspective and to keep Him first. The conclusion of the matter rests in our ability to maintain proper balance in our responsibilities to God, our families, and our brothers and sisters. It's all a balancing act.

Chapter 9 - Helicopters and Airplanes

"The word of God, you see, is alive and moving; sharper than a double-edged sword; piercing the divide between soul and spirit, joints and marrow; able to judge the thoughts and will of the heart." Hebrews 4:12

Helicopters and airplanes are both methods of transportation by air. They both have their own unique purpose and at the same time, their unique limitations. When properly employed and utilized, their functionality is matchless. A helicopter cannot begin to compete with the speed of an airplane. An airplane could not land or set itself down on a pad like a helicopter can. Amid the other unique features one has over the other, that does not render one more important than the other, just a different purpose.

"And when he had called unto him his twelve disciples, he gave them power against unclean spirits, to cast them out, and to heal all manner of sickness and all manner of disease."
Matthew 10:1

When Jesus called His disciples, He called 12 ordinary individuals with uniquely different personalities, backgrounds, and occupations, and yet they were given the same assignment. He equipped them with the same power to accomplish the assignment, but the methods used to accomplish it did not have to be identical. That has not changed even today. This same God uses ordinary people but the same Holy Spirit to empower and equip disciples today to fulfill their God-given assignment.

I began my apprenticeship with about 24 others. Our future job responsibilities were all the same. We all varied in age, gender, and culture. We were required to complete the same core classes designed to develop us into future journeymen. There were 5 different worksites that could be assigned to us.

Once our apprenticeship was completed, we would be assigned to a construction, production, Press Metal operation, building maintenance, or Engineering/Administration Office area. Each area required a particular skillset that was necessary for maintaining that area. Because we had no idea where we would end up, upon completion, we were required to learn and develop all of the skills necessary for each.

I must admit, I was a little intimidated early on because some of the apprentices seemed to show greater skill and aptitude than I did in some areas. As I rotated to different areas, I discovered that I performed better than others as well. After getting to know some of the journeymen a little more, they shared with me that no journeyman possessed exceptional skills in every aspect of the trade. They explained it was the reason we work as a team.

When we work together in our special skillset, we get the optimal results as a unit. I thought about the military, the medical field, and ultimately, the church; they operate under the same principles. That's why we have 4 divisions of the military. That's why we have medical specialists, each serving with the same goal in mind but from their own unique specialty.

I later discovered a very similar model within the church and its ministries. We all have (or should have) the same goals in mind: winning souls to Christ, encouraging those that have accepted the gift of salvation, and utilizing the uniqueness of each individual disciple of Christ. I now realize that sometimes I am better served as a worker, sometimes as a facilitator, and sometimes as an administrator. Whatever the capacity, the end result is what matters most.

Helicopters have been around since 1861. They are referred to as helicopters, choppers, helos, copters, and whirlybirds. Helicopters are much noisier than planes. They have two rotors (one on top and one on the tail). They provide the ability for it to lift vertically into the air. There is a nut that holds the main rotor to the shaft of the helicopter, and it's called the "Jesus Nut." Although helicopters cannot travel as fast as planes, they serve countless valuable purposes.

- They are often used to transport medical emergencies

because they can sit down on building tops.

- They are often used to fight fires because they can set over the problem area and dump de-accelerants on the fires.

- They are often used to capture aerial photographs.

- They are occasionally used in a Police chase or search operation.

- We used them quite often, as others do, to remove or set rooftop air handling units.

You may or may not know of other uses, but either way, you can see that helicopters serve many useful purposes.

Airplanes cannot be safely utilized for those purposes, at least, not in the same manner. An airplane might be used to transport a medical emergency long distance. They might be used to fly over fires and spray the area as they travel over it. There may even be examples of photographs taken from a plane, but these would be very unique situations, such as military surveillance.

Airplanes require a runway to lift off. Some need less distance than others, but they all require one. They can generally transport more passengers than a helicopter. They can travel further than a helicopter. Lastly, and very importantly, they must have some sort of runway for safe landing. So, what's the point?

For this illustration, the point is that first of all, everything that we see or know to be in existence or ever will be, God created it. John 1:1-3 reminds us,

"In the beginning was the Word, and the Word was with God, and the Word was God. He was with God in the beginning. <u>All things were created through Him, and apart from Him not one thing was created that has been created.</u>"

Mankind and the things produced by, through and from man, all fall into the category of things God created. Man can only make things from the resources that God has already provided through creation. The one common goal, central to both man and things is the objective intended use that each should be to glorify God.

In the book of Genesis (Chapters 1-3), we discover the purpose of God's creation. God desired to be in relationship with Adam and Eve, as He does with us, and He gave Adam dominion over all of His created beings. They were told to be fruitful and multiply. They were not told to be greedy, controlling, uncaring, unappreciative, or destructive. Nevertheless, here we are.

God created everything that exists *with* a purpose and *for* a purpose. Ultimately, His purpose is to be praised, worshiped, and glorified by His creation. This is not necessarily carried out the exact same way by each of His created entities, but it is nevertheless an expectation of God. Since God has placed that expectation, it is possible or doable. So, why are there so many struggling to give God not only what He desires but also what He so deserves? We too often seek inward results from outward measures.

I John 2:16 explains it this way. He says,

"For everything that belongs to the world, the lust of the flesh, the lust of the eyes, and the pride in one's lifestyle is not from the Father, but is from the world."

Aside from utilizing ourselves for the glory of God, we pursue the things of this world for satisfaction and contentment. If we have the 5 physical senses that God created us with, we should use them to discover and develop the spiritual sensitivity God provides us. When these are working in unison, the 5 physical senses become an asset to our spiritual development. When we do not, we align ourselves with the desires of the world.

What does that look like? Well, we find ourselves seeking material things for spiritual tranquility. We see this played out in many different forms, but most often it shows up in modeling the behavior of the world.

The purpose for God calling people into ministry is to introduce, inform, and equip the lost with the way of salvation and to reassure those that are saved that our only real hope for fulfilling our purpose is in Christ. Everyone that's lost will not receive the good news of the gospel the same way. Each of us has differing learning modes and receptors. While it is true that the Holy Spirit is the one that opens the mind to see, believe, understand, and accept the invitation to accept the gift of salvation, lost people utilize their 5 physical senses first.

Dean Williams, one of my Bible college professors shared an experience he had in the military while serving as a chaplain. He told us about an occasion where they had been ambushed and several soldiers were critically wounded. Their job as chaplains was to find the wounded, assess the severity of their wounds, and then administer medical treatment.

On this occasion, he observed one chaplain attending to a severely wounded soldier. The soldier kept saying, "I'm cold, I'm cold." The chaplain thought, as he stood over the soldier, "I don't think he is going to make it." Then he took out his Bible and asked the soldier if there was a particular passage of scripture he could read to him. The soldier replied, "Get away from me. I don't want you to do anything for me." So, the chaplain walked away and moved on to another soldier.

Dean Williams walked over to the soldier, and before saying a word, he found something like a backpack and placed it under the wounded soldier's head. He then gave him a drink from his canteen. He took his coat off and put it over the soldier's cold body. He then asked the soldier if he had a favorite scripture that he could read to him. The soldier responded, "If there's something in that book that made you do what you did, you can read any passage to me." He concluded that story with these words: while it is true that everyone needs the spiritual word of the gospel for survival, a hungry man will not listen to you until his physical needs are met.

All people and situations are different. The methods we use in ministry will often vary based on the situation. Yes, we learn from apprenticing or being mentored by other ministry leaders with more experience, but we don't or we shouldn't mimic their behavior. We must develop a relationship with the God that motivates, guides, equips, and instructs the servant.

During my early years in ministry, I observed the elders around me. I asked questions sometimes, and other times I just made mental notes. It was so easy to get caught up in a mindset of performance rather than ministry. I wanted to be the best I could be, and we were always pointed to the big-name preachers around the country as people to observe, study, and pattern our craft after. I thank God that He placed older, seasoned, and mature pastors around me. So many young preachers didn't have that luxury, and it was reflected in their development, or lack thereof.

Rather than copying the behaviors of other great men of God, I tried to learn from them. What I discovered is that God instills different gifts in different people and for different reasons. They each have special assignments. Paul says at I Corinthians 12:4-11,

> *Now there are different gifts, but the same Spirit. There are different ministries, but the same Lord. And there are different activities, but the same God activates each gift in each person. A demonstration of the Spirit is given to each person to produce what is beneficial:*
> - *to one is given a message of wisdom through the Spirit,*
> - *to another, a message of knowledge by the same Spirit,*
> - *to another, faith by the same Spirit,*
> - *to another, gifts of healing by the one Spirit,*
> - *to another, the performing of miracles,*
> - *to another, prophecy,*
> - *to another, distinguishing between spirits,*
> - *to another, different kinds of languages,*
> - *to another, interpretation of languages.*
>
> *But one and the same Spirit is active in all these, distributing to each person as He wills.*

I place these contrasting gifts into two categories: *Helicopters and Airplanes*. Some of them require the ability to rise up instantly, and minister to the needs of those God has assigned to them. Others require more patience and time. They are like airplanes. They need a runway to get off the ground and fulfill their assignment. Each is unique in its own way, but God determines who is assigned what.

He knows which assignment is best for us. Our responsibility is to continuously pursue a relationship with Him that enables us to discover whether our calling pattern is more suited to a helicopter-like behavior or an airplane, then function appropriately in that capacity.

Chapter 10 - Processing It All

"Really, what profit is there for you to gain the whole world and lose yourself in the process? What can you give in exchange for your life?" Mark 8:36-37

It usually takes about 3-4 rotations during an apprenticeship to begin to see certain required skills developing within an apprentice. There are a number of factors that go into that equation. The novice apprentice usually begins his learning by focusing on the necessary skills needed to perform the work.

If an apprentice is fortunate enough to be assigned to a journeyman that takes pride in transferring knowledge and skill to his apprentice, the end result is generally productive. No apprentice is going to pick up every detail in one rotation, but each opportunity to ask questions helps you to gain understanding of what you are doing and why, providing an environment for encouragement and growth.

If you are assigned to a journeyman that either has a low skill set himself or very little interest in teaching, that apprentice is in for a long 6 months. I had my share of both. I discussed in Chapter 8 the importance of balance. At times like these, a wise apprentice implements balance. To be effective in balancing your environment, you must develop effective processing skills. Processing, in its basic sense, is to receive input and provide the appropriate output. That might seem like an easy task if you simply do the math. One could take their 6 months, divide it into 40 hour weeks, and project an end date. Once that is completed, you could then focus on the end date, one day at a time.

If you had a journeyman that enjoyed teaching and sharing, those six months would seem to go by faster. If you, on the other hand, had a journeyman that didn't really seem to have any interest in developing you, those six months would seem like a lifetime. An apprentice needs to be perceptively careful in his actions. If you asked too many questions or showed too much ambition in your work, you might offend some journeymen. If you were too laid back, you might be labeled as lazy, uninterested, or unfit.

As simple as this may sound, the most favorable approach for an apprentice is to assess the personality and skill set of the journeyman you're assigned to and then establish an approach to learning that will maximize your effort. It seems a simple process but often times involve complicated implementation. Sometimes, the best of efforts fail because of conflicting personalities.

Jesus chose 12 disciples, each with differing personalities. He taught them all in the same manner, and yet they all learned at a different pace and at varying levels of understanding. While Jesus didn't show a difference in how He interacted with them, He did have a closer relationship with three of the 12: Peter, James, and John. Most scholars refer to them as His inner circle. They were no better than the other nine; they just seemed to have a closer relationship with Him. Perhaps it was because they were the first disciples He called and they had been with Him longer.

John MacArthur, in his book *"Twelve Ordinary Men,"* points out that Jesus grouped the disciples into three groups of four. The closer group was Peter, James, John and Andrew. The second group was Phillip, Bartholomew, Matthew and Thomas. The last group was James, Simon, Thaddeus and Judas. Again, not one of them was better or treated better than the other, but the four disciples in the first group had a closer relationship with Jesus.

The four disciples in the first group had something in common that might have fashioned them more unique than the others. They were two groups of brothers and they were all fishermen. James and John were brothers and Andrew and Peter were brothers. Maybe they were more capable of processing and comprehending the parables Jesus taught them by utilizing analogies of fishing. Whatever the reason, the truth remains, these four were His inner circle.

Jesus reveals a valuable example for us. Although we may be closer to some in our circle than others, we must treat them all with the same degree of care and respect. Paul speaks to this point at Colossians 4:5-6,

"Use your heads as you live and work among others, close and not so close. Make the most of every opportunity. Be gracious in your speech. The goal is to bring out the best in others in conversation, not put them down, not cut them out."

There were some 6-month periods when certain apprentices did not rotate. When large projects were going on or about to begin, additional apprentices would be maintained for extra manpower. If you rotated to a project area such as this, you would often encounter journeymen that were more engaged with apprentices that had been with them 6 months prior. If you didn't know that, you could easily think that they were shunning or slighting you for no reason. That's just another reason why you must process each situation that you find yourself in. Preferring one apprentice over another might not be the right thing to do, but people are different and sometimes we just click or connect better with some people than others. It is much less stressful when you are able to constructively and productively process the decisions occurring around you.

When Jesus established the three groups within His disciples, there is no record of one group complaining or questioning why one person was in a particular group. Andrew was called before his brother, Peter, and ironically, it was Peter that became the accepted leader among the disciples. In fact, Andrew wasn't always included with the other three. When Jesus took disciples with Him to the Mountain of Transfiguration and in the heart of the Garden of Gethsemane, He took Peter, James and John only. No where do we find Andrew complaining or questioning Jesus or the other disciples about not being included. It's all about how you process what's happening around you.

Effective processing is similar to effective statistics. One Statistics professor used to remind us before we began our research, "Don't determine your outcome, and then look for data to support it." Unfortunately, there are studies even today that reflect those kinds of results. Effective processing requires the processor to identify the actual issues, verify their validity, search diligently and thoroughly for pertinent historical and contemporary data, measure and test the results, implement a model, and manage the model for adjustment and success.

When I look back over that period of time, I see countless examples of men that aided me in properly processing my environment and the many aspects of what was going on. There were many times where I would have improperly processed what I thought I saw. They would pull me aside and explain what was really happening and why. I can only imagine where I might have been today if I had been left to my own imagination.

I relate many of those experiences with those of the

disciples. So many times, they would have the wrong understanding of something Jesus said or did, and He would pull them aside or take them to a place where He could gather their undivided attention and explain what He did or said and what it meant. One of those occasions occurred in the 9th Chapter of the Gospel of Mark. A man brought his son to the disciples hoping they would expel an unclean spirit from his son, but they could not. When the man saw Jesus and explained what had happened and asked if Jesus could help his son. Jesus told the man, *"All things are possible if you can believe."* Jesus commanded the unclean spirit to come out of the boy, and it did. At verses 28-29, we read,

"Later He and His disciples gathered privately in a house. The disciples asked Jesus: Why couldn't we cast out that unclean spirit? Jesus said that sort of powerful spirit can only be conquered with much prayer and fasting." Mark 9:28-29

Sometimes we can become so caught up with *what* we see that we fail to understand the complexity of *how* some things happen. All followers of Christ are His disciples. Our ability to process and utilize the power that He provides us is ultimately predicated on our relationship with Him. In relationship, we understand that every victory we experience in ministry is dependent on and accomplished through His Holy Spirit. While it may have seemed a simple task when they observed Jesus performing miracles of healing, Jesus only healed when it was in alignment with His father's will and for His Father's glory.

"And whatsoever ye shall ask in my name, that will I do, that the Father may be glorified in the Son." John 14:13

I understand that people use various methods to guide their decisions. For those that choose not to follow the biblical example, they have that right. Their options may be based on statistics, past practices, or a gut feeling; it's still their right. It took me some years of conditioning to come to the conclusion that in all aspects of life, it's my relationship with God that makes the difference.

"Trust in the LORD with all your heart, and do not rely on your own understanding; think about Him in all your ways, and He will guide you on the right paths." Proverbs 3:5-6

When I process the fundamentals of my life, I must personally expand beyond a biblical view only. I have to seriously assess all of the components that create the reality of my life. Historical conditioning, socio-economic challenges, cultural differences, societal framing, typing, and perceptions all play a role in how I perceive things and how I am perceived. I place the greatest weight on my Christian perspective, not just because I see it as the great equalizer among mankind, but I truly believe that God and His written requirements and directions are man's only real hope.

During my apprenticeship, it took a number of years to fully comprehend the unfairness, the injustice, the politics, and several other improprieties that contributed to an uneven playing field. Processing these findings revealed to me that an even playing field was never the intention. The great disparity within the interviewing, testing, and selection process was never intended to be fair, equal, and equitable. It was designed to provide certain people easy access into the program while making it extremely difficult (sometimes impossible) for others to get in. I experienced at least 3 occasions where attempts were stringently pursued to remove apprentices after they were in the program; I was one of the three.

Processing is not always just about understanding. For so many, it is about understanding what's going on around you and finding the means to ultimately realize a successful outcome while you navigate waters that are sprinkled with sharks, gators, and piranhas. This is probably not what you thought and certainly not what you wanted to hear, but it is true reality for the less dominate culture in most areas of life.

Now if you're thinking, "that's why he leans so heavily on Biblical Principles," you're partially correct. As I mentioned earlier, *The Bible* is the great equalizer. Nevertheless, the church still has a lot of work to do. Our churches are still some of the most segregated organizations and institutions in our world. We are in agreement that the message presented in scripture is the best antidote for healing the ills of society, but that message is presented in too many instances with great imbalance.

God's people during Old Testament times had to endure the oppression of neighboring people. The "ites" of old (the Amalekites, the Amorites, the Jebusites, the Hittites, the Girgasites, the Hivites, the Arkites, the Sinites, the Arvadites, the Zemarites, the Hamathites, and the families of the Canaanites) all played a very significant role in displaying this. Jesus even had to deal with oppression, depression, hate, schemes, and political structures that sought to impede His progress. It ultimately led to His death on the cross, but His battle did not end there. Rather, His and our victory began there.

After Jesus was crucified, He appeared to the disciples in an upper room. It was there that He said to Thomas,

"Because you have seen Me, you have believed. Those who believe without seeing are blessed." Jesus performed many other signs in the presence of His disciples that are not written in this book. But these are written so that you may believe Jesus is the Messiah, the Son of God, and by believing you may have life in His name.
John 19:29-30

It is for that reason that I declare the Bible as the great equalizer. I know this is a lot to process, but it's the truth. I understand that the natural mind is unable to receive this message, but for those who submit to and allow the Holy Spirit to instruct them, it is good news. It's the only way our world will experience deliverance. Can you process this?

"However, if my people, who are called by my name, will humble themselves, pray, search for me, and turn from their evil ways, then I will hear their prayer from heaven, forgive their sins, and heal their country." II Chronicles 7:14

Chapter 11 - It's all about the Journey

"The L<small>ORD</small> your God is testing you to find out if you really love him with all your heart and with all your soul." Deuteronomy 13:3

I'm not certain when it happened, but some say it occurred during the invention of the microwave oven. I'm speaking to the heightened level of impatience that exists today. Most of us are passionate in our pursuit to discover our purpose, our goals, and what we consider success. Those are good, if not great pursuits; however, the manner in which so many implement them and the methods utilized to achieve them, scream impatience.

Certainly, it's not because that particular achievement creates a permanent place of contentment. For most, it seems like as soon as one level is acquired, a new pursuit is instantly on the horizon.

You may recall the offer Jesus made to the potential disciples in Chapter 7, *"Follow Me, and I will make you to "become" fishers of men."* Not make you, or make you into, or make you overnight, but make you to become, fishers of men. It's a process and maybe more important than reaching the status is the journey while getting there. I think *it's all about the journey.*

I entered into an apprenticeship program in the late 1970s.

We were told that the program usually takes 4 years to complete. The 4 years were calculated using a 40 hour week. If we were willing to work extra hours when offered, we could complete it sooner. At first I thought, "No, 40 hours is enough for me." About a year later, I found myself like most other apprentices working all of the extra hours offered. We wanted to complete the program as fast as we could because journeyman pay was a lot more than apprentice pay. After all, obtaining that Journeyman's Card was the objective, right?

I remember working so many hours at times I didn't know what day of the week it was. I knew what day payday was, and I could hardly wait to see how much I had made by putting in those extra hours. It seemed like no matter how much I got paid, I was still looking for more. One day, I thought about what an older gentleman told me about money. He said, *"How much you make is not as important as how much you keep."* It took some years for me to really grasp what he was saying, but I thank God that he said it. I didn't fully understand it at the time, but it remained on my mind. God has placed people of wisdom around me throughout my life. I didn't always accept what they said, but the seed was planted. Once a seed is planted, it has an opportunity to grow and develop.

"Don't become like the people of this world. Instead, change the way you think. Then you will always be able to determine what God really wants—what is good, pleasing, and perfect."

Romans 12:2

About a year ago, I was blessed to be able to take a trip to the Holy Land. A trip to the land where Jesus walked, taught and gave His life for us has always been at the top of my list of trips. It took a lot of planning, preparation and sacrifice, but no trip I've ever taken compares to that trip. I had all sorts of ideas about that land, what I would do when I got there and the places I wanted to see. While I did have the opportunity to see all of those sites, the journey itself is what has meant the most to me. It was all about the journey.

I had to be taken to a nearby shuttle service, which took me to a city 2 hours away. From there, I took a flight to Canada where I had a 6 hour layover. From Toronto, Canada, we took a flight to Israel. I was part of a group of 16 from different parts of Tennessee. A better group of people could not have been created. The entire trip was glitch free. It was so amazing to see, touch, and feel the presence of God, everywhere we went. We even connected with a group of young college mission students. That brought about a sense of comfort, knowing that the next generation was being prepared and equipped to continue the Great Commission given by Jesus at Matthew 28:19-20,

"Then Jesus came near and said to them, "All authority has been given to Me in heaven and on earth. Go, therefore, and make disciples of all nations, baptizing them in the name of the Father and of the Son and of the Holy Spirit, teaching them to observe

everything I have commanded you. And remember, I am with you always, to the end of the age."

We shared experiences, fellowship, and prayer with them, far into the night. It became obvious that they were enjoying the time spent with us as much as we were enjoying time with them. It was a very busy trip. Our tour guide had planned a route throughout the region that exposed us to countless biblical accounts and sites. The cultural differences of the natives were very educational and humbling.

My brother-in-law and I roomed together. Each night we would discuss the magnitude of our day's experience and what it meant to us. We both thought nothing could top what we had experienced that day. The next day, our new experiences were just as intriguing as the day before. Connecting the Scriptures with the visual was just amazing.

"Now unto Him who is able to carry out His purpose and do superabundantly more than all that we dare ask or think infinitely beyond our greatest prayers, hopes, or dreams, according to His power that is at work within us," Ephesians 3:20

Life, no matter what stage you are in, is a process of progression. We are all evolving or developing into the person we will become. As long as there is life in the body, some sort of growth is occurring. There are some phases of that process that I relished more than others, but collectively, they are ultimately producing a finished product. I am so thankful that I am not alone in this or totally responsible for completing this finished product.

God uses His influence (The Holy Spirit) to move us along this process. Sometimes, He pushes us forward when we are slothful, sometimes He holds us back when we are moving too fast or approaching danger, and sometimes He allows us to move around, seemingly in circles, until we develop the character and trust necessary to appreciate God's involvement in our lives.

The children of Israel are one example of God's hand in accomplishing His will, even if He has to weed out some people. Numbers 32:11-13 says,

"Even though that particular land had been promised to the Israelites beginning with Abraham, then to Isaac and to Jacob after him, the whole generation that left Egypt when they were 20 years or older would have to die, wandering aimlessly in the desert, before God would allow the community to enter that great land. Only Caleb the Kenizzite (Jephunneh's son) and Joshua (Nun's son) out of that generation would be allowed to enjoy settlement there because they followed Him completely."

If your trek through life is like most, there have been many chapters throughout your journey where you could hardly wait to get through a particular part of what was before you. If you had a specific target you were aiming for, it probably made that delay or impediment even more challenging. After getting through that struggle, you probably questioned, "Why did I have such a hard time with this?"

For me, I spent a lot of time interrogating myself. Am I making the decision? Am I fully applying myself? Should I be doing this or something else? What would someone else in my situation do? All of these were reasonable questions, but my focus should have been on my target or goal.

Andy Stanley, in his book, *The Principle of the Path,* helped me with this dilemma. He repeatedly explained what I consider the theme of his book: Direction, not desire, determines destiny. He simplified this idea by conveying a thought that if your intention is to travel to a location that is east of where you are, traveling west would never get you there, no matter how strong your desire to get there is. We must do our best to focus on and move in the direction of our pursuit, or we will never make it. I found this to be a very powerful piece of advice. Especially for Disciples of Christ, when we put our energy into becoming what God wants us to be, utilizing the tools and experiences that He provides us, He will assist us in getting there.

"Being confident of this very thing, that he who hath begun a

good work in you will perform it until the day of Jesus Christ:"
Philippians 1:6

As mentioned earlier, for the believer, the Christian life is a progressive one. We don't one day arrive at a place in life and assert, "I have arrived!" When an Olympic runner enters a race, he may have spent countless hours training and preparing. His intention is to cross the finish line first because his desire is to win. If he wins, he's not done. He celebrates the victory and begins training for the next race. It's the same way with life victories in the faith, and you don't have to be in the Olympics to do it.

When we accomplish goals in life, we celebrate them and then reconnect with our trainer (The Holy Spirit) to receive our next set of instructions for the next race. Each victory prepares us for the next one. We apply certain parts or elements of past races or victories to our new assignment, and that produces confidence, assurance, and a host of other nuggets that give us the push we need to continue progressing forward. The experiences that we look back on are not for bragging rights, they are the building blocks for the next journey.

I remember when I finished my first apprentice period and rotated. There was a sense of pride, but more than that, I now believed that I could get through this program. I had data to support and prove it. I wish I could say that every rotation was that way, but it wasn't. There were times when the work environment was horrible for six months. On one or two occasions, the classes that I was taking were horrifying. It was during those times that I would think back on other periods that I had gotten through, and that enabled me to persevere.

I think back on the time I decided to take a full load of classes because the work hours were low, and I thought I could get ahead. In the middle of that period, another apprentice and I were transferred to a different site where we had to work 84 hours a week. I wondered how I was going to get through those classes. I no longer had time to spend with tutors, and the coursework in physics was very challenging. My new journeyman noticed me studying during one of my breaks and asked how it was going. I told him it was physics and that I was struggling with it. As it turned out, he was working on his engineering degree and physics was his favorite subject. He showed me some simple ways to structure formulas and calculate solutions, and I finished that course with ease.

For most of my eight-period program, I thought it was all about getting my apprenticeship completed and receiving my Journeyman's Card. I paid little attention to the relationships that were being forged. Every now and again I come across a former journeyman that I worked with, or I receive a phone call from someone that made a huge difference in my life. I now realize that God had not only placed me in certain places during these times but had also placed certain people there to support and guide me.

God shows the same kind of concern with His disciples. He displayed it with the 12 disciples He placed under Jesus's tutorship. He revealed it with countless numbers of people in the Old Testament, and He does it now with the many Christian disciples throughout the world, unmatched by any mentorship any of us have ever experienced. When He gives an assignment, especially the ones that are too big for us, He places others in our circle to assist us in getting the assignment completed. All He ever asks is that we look back over our journey and garner assurance as we reflect over the previous journeys that He has successfully brought us through. He never sends us to a situation without providing the necessities to get us through it.

From Genesis 22, Abraham had a son, Isaac. God tested Abraham by telling him to sacrifice Isaac. At the most critical point, God provided an acceptable sacrifice and spared Isaac's life. Abraham's faith was strengthened as a result of that journey.

"And they came to the place which God had told him of; and Abraham built an altar there, and laid the wood in order, and bound Isaac his son, and laid him on the altar upon the wood. And Abraham stretched forth his hand, and took the knife to slay his son. And the angel of the LORD called unto him out of heaven, and said, Abraham, Abraham: and he said, Here am I. And he said, Lay not thine hand upon the lad, neither do thou

anything unto him: for now I know that thou fearest God, seeing thou hast not withheld thy son, thine only son from me. And Abraham lifted up his eyes, and looked, and behold behind him a ram caught in a thicket by his horns: and Abraham went and took the ram, and offered him up for a burnt offering in the stead of his son." Genesis 22:9-13

When God sent Moses to Egypt with instructions to tell Pharaoh to let His people go, Moses told God he couldn't do it because of a speech impediment. God told him to take Aaron with him as a spokesperson.

"And Moses told Aaron all the words of the Lord who had sent him, and all the signs which he had commanded him."
Exodus 4:28

"And afterward Moses and Aaron went in, and told Pharaoh, Thus saith the Lord God of Israel, Let my people go, that they may hold a feast unto me in the wilderness."
Exodus 5:1

Goliath was wreaking havoc with Saul's army, and his men were afraid and stymied. God sent and equipped David to conquer Goliath.

'And the Philistine said, I defy the armies of Israel this day; give me a man, that we may fight together. When Saul and all Israel

heard those words of the Philistine, they were dismayed, and greatly afraid. And all the men of Israel, when they saw the man, fled from him, and were sore afraid. And David spoke to the men that stood by him, saying, What shall be done to the man that kills this Philistine, and take away this reproach from Israel? For who is this uncircumcised Philistine, that he should defy the armies of the living God? And David said to Saul, Let no man's heart fail because of him; your servant will go and fight with this Philistine. Your servant slew both a lion and a bear: and this uncircumcised Philistine shall be as one of them, seeing he hath defied the armies of the living God. And David put his hand in his bag, and took out a stone, and slung it, and struck the Philistine in his forehead. That stone sunk into his forehead; and he fell upon his face to the ground. So David prevailed over the Philistine with a sling and with a stone, and smote the Philistine, and slew him; but there was no sword in the hand of David."
I Samuel 17:10-11, 24, 26, 32, 36 & 49-50

When Paul (Saul) encountered Jesus on the Damascus road and was convicted and blinded, he was sent to Cornelius to have his sight restored.

"Saul was given papers from the high priest so that if he found any men or women who belonged to the faith, he might bring them as prisoners to Jerusalem. As he traveled and was nearing

Damascus, a light from heaven suddenly flashed around him. Falling to the ground, he heard a voice saying to him, "Saul, Saul, why are you persecuting Me?" "Who are You, Lord?" he said. "I am Jesus, the One you are persecuting," He replied. "But get up and go into the city, and you will be told what you must do." The men who were traveling with him stood speechless, hearing the sound but seeing no one. Then Saul got up from the ground, and though his eyes were open, he could see nothing. So they took him by the hand and led him into Damascus. He was unable to see for three days and did not eat or drink. Saul was sent to a disciple in Damascus named Ananias. And the Lord said to him in a vision, "Ananias!" "Get up and go to the street called Straight," "to the house of Judas, and ask for a man from Tarsus named Saul, since he is praying there. In a vision he has seen a man named Ananias coming in and placing his hands on him so he can regain his sight." "Go! For this man is My chosen vessel to take My name to Gentiles, kings, and the Israelites. I will show him how much he must suffer for My name!" So Ananias left and entered the house. Then he placed his hands on him and said, "Brother Saul, the Lord Jesus, who appeared to you on the road you were traveling, has sent me so that you can regain your sight and be filled with the Holy Spirit." At once something like scales fell from his eyes, and he regained his sight." Acts 9:2-18

There are numerous examples throughout scripture where God has placed people in the paths of others. Sometimes it is to strengthen their faith and sometimes it is to redirect their path. It is always, however, to fulfill God's purpose and will and to assist them in completing a mission or assignment.

Statistics show that championship series (best 2 out of 3 or best 4 out of 7) are most often won by the team that wins the first game. It doesn't happen because they are the better or most talented team but because the confidence that a team develops after a win, more often than not, produces an insurmountable challenge. I agree that the wins, the championships, the trophies, and all the whoopla that comes with it, are certainly satisfying and gratifying. However, in reality, when all of the dust settles and real value is proportioned, it doesn't matter if it's an apprenticeship program or a program of ministry; "It's all about the journey."

Chapter 12 - Souled Out

At Mark 12:30, Jesus said,

"And thou shalt love the Lord thy God with all thy heart, and <u>with all thy soul</u>, and with all thy mind, and with all thy strength: this is the first commandment."

It is from these words that I surmise what He desires; it is for all of His followers to be sold out or souled out for the cause of Christ. The cause of Christ is that we would follow His instructions given at Matthew 28:19-20,

"Go out and make disciples in all the nations. Ceremonially wash them through baptism in the name of the triune God: Father, Son, and Holy Spirit. Then disciple them. Form them in the practices and postures that I have taught you, and show them how to follow the commands I have laid down for you. And I will be with you, day after day, to the end of the age."

Within this chapter I will define the concept of "Souled Out," what it suggests, and what it does not.

Being souled out for the Lord does not imply that one is perfect in terms of flawlessness. It does not convey the idea that every other word that proceeds from our mouths must be "Praise the Lord, Hallelujah, What would Jesus do, or God is good, all the time, and all the time, God is good." While all of these phrases are good and true, they may not resonate with everyone that you meet in life. God's desire is that we reflect the love and presence of God in our daily walk and encourage others to come to know the God that extends the same unconditional love to people of all walks of life.

One question that is so often asked is, "If God is so good and loving, why does He allow so many terrible things to happen to good people?" As I write this chapter, the world is struggling with the devastation of a coronavirus that is taking the lives of the rich and poor, the young and old, Christians and non-Christians, black, brown, yellow, white, male, and female. No one is exempt from its fury.

When a young ruler addressed Jesus as "good Master," he also asked Him "what *good* thing he could do, that he might have eternal life. This was Jesus's response,

"Strange that you should ask Me what is good. There is only One who is good. If you want to participate in His divine life, obey the Commandments." Matthew 19:17

There is no one good enough to earn or deserve eternal life. Eternal life is about having a relationship with God and accepting His Son, Jesus Christ, and the atoning sacrifice He made for His followers. We all, in every category listed earlier, are good enough to deserve death because that's what sin earns. Romans 6:23 reminds us that,

> *"The wages of sin is death; but the gift of God is eternal life through Jesus Christ our Lord."*

Unless we accept the shed blood of Jesus as a covering for our sin, no good that we do is good enough to atone for our sin condition. When we do good deeds, it is the spirit of God that initiates them. The Word of God at Matthew 5:16 tells us,

> *"You are like that illuminating light. Let your light shine everywhere you go, that you may illumine creation, so men and women everywhere may see your good actions, may see creation at its fullest, may see your devotion to Me, and may turn and praise your Father In heaven because of it."*

It's not that good things happen to bad people or bad things happen to good people; things, good and bad happen to people, period. What we do in light of our experiences is what really matters.

The person that is 100% souled out for the Lord processes his experiences differently than the rest. He's no better than others, but his perspective is immersed in the will of God. Bad experiences hurt, bother, affect, and trouble just as it does anyone else, but they don't destroy or crush. Paul said at II Corinthians 4:8-10,

"We are troubled on every side, yet not distressed; we are perplexed, but not in despair; Persecuted, but not forsaken; cast down, but not destroyed; Always bearing about in the body the dying of the Lord Jesus, that the life also of Jesus might be made manifest in our body."

Being souled out for the Lord is not easily attained, and it does not happen overnight. It does, however, happen for those that continue to walk closely with the Lord. It requires a mindset of commitment. Isaiah 26:3 assures us,

"Thou wilt keep him in perfect peace, whose mind is stayed on thee: because he continuously trusts in Me."

We sometimes believe we have to reach a certain level of doing to be worthy of God's love. That is far from the truth. Our behavior, no matter how exemplary, will never make us worthy of His love. God loves us unconditionally and completely. Good or bad, no one can reverse or change God's love for us. It is an eternal transaction. Jeremiah 31:2b-3 encourages us with these words.

"When Israel went in search of rest, I appeared to them from far away and said: "I have loved you with an everlasting love, out of faithfulness I have drawn you close."

That is great news for all of us. Our accomplishments as Christians, have no bearing on God's love for us. In fact, we are all reminded at John 3:16-17 that,

"For God loved the world in this way: He gave His One and Only Son, so that everyone who believes in Him will not perish but have eternal life. For God did not send His Son into the world that He might condemn the world, but that the world might be saved through Him."

God expects us to model the love that He shows toward us to the world around us. We accomplish this by using what He has infused into us to make a positive impact on the world. That's why it is so important that we develop and maintain a close relationship with Him. It is during those times that He reveals our calling and gifting. Once discovered, we are to use those qualities to provide light in darkness and seasoning in a sometimes tasteless environment.

A mindset of our future reward in heaven should be enough to urge and encourage Christians to continue working for the Lord. Jesus Christ is the ultimate reward for those who do not give up on God's work. The writer of Hebrews 12, Verses 1-2 says to us,

"Let us lay aside every weight and the sin that so easily ensnares us. Let us run with endurance the race that lies before us, keeping our eyes on Jesus, the source, and perfecter, of our faith,"

Unlike anyone you've ever met in life, God calls and draws us to an assignment that He enables us to accomplish by supplying everything or every person we need to complete it. You won't find that in the best of friends. While all of this is going on, He is perfecting our faith.

"Be strong therefore, and don't let your hands become weak: for your work shall be rewarded." II Chronicles 15:7

When you are souled out for the Lord, you won't have to tell anyone, it will speak for itself. Be aware, however, that some will be irritated by your level of commitment. Be aware, but don't be angered or frustrated. A souled out position is a category that you grow into, and not everyone is willing to make sacrifices that it requires. That's why it necessitates patience. God will assist anyone who sincerely desires growth. Keep in mind though, the motivation behind the desire has consequences.

"Woe to you, you teachers of the law and Pharisees. What you say is not what you do. You steal the homes from under the widows while you pretend to pray for them. You will suffer great condemnation for this." Matthew 23:14

Developing a souled out mentality is certainly not predicated on only reflecting about what God has done in our lives, but it does help. We cannot repay God for the blessings He bestows on us. We can, however, show our appreciation. All that God has done in guiding, protecting, and providing in our lives is part of His providential nature. He certainly doesn't have to do any of those things, but we are so much better off because of His love for us and the care He continuously provides, even when we are unaware of the things He's doing.

There are many more times that God has moved on my behalf than are indicated in this book. That being said, the experiences mentioned are more than enough to warrant my commitment to Him. Although that level of commitment wasn't there during many of those encounters, I thank Him for sustaining my life and affording me the opportunity to show how much I appreciate Him. I'm sure you can look back over your life and find times when nobody but God delivered you from situations in which you found yourself. My prayer is that you too, will see those experiences as additional reasons to be souled out for the Lord.

In Chapter 1, I talk about *Our Divine Purpose*. It is God that plants His purpose in us. How awesome is that? God invites and utilizes finite humans to carry-out His divine purposes. If you remember, I explained how God designed each one of us with talents, skills, and specific abilities that no one else has. It is incumbent upon us to position ourselves around the people that He has placed in our path to assist us in the development of those abilities. Once matured, we are released to fulfill our purpose. The fulfilling of our purpose impacts our lives and the environment around us. Most importantly, fulfilling our purpose creates an agency relationship between God and us that usher in, His will.

Chapter 2, *Angel at the Door*, shares an encounter I had as a child, where my mother allowed a stranger into our home (that she later believed was an angel) who anointed me for God's purpose. I am not encouraging anyone to arbitrarily open their door to strangers, but on this particular day, I believe the Holy Spirit moved my mother to do what she never would do, and yet she responded correctly. According to the scriptures, we have all entertained angels, unaware. Even though I can't prove it, there have been other occasions where God has dispatched angels to protect us, and we never knew they were present. I wonder what new experiences I would be sharing if my mother had not opened the door.

In Chapter 3, I shared my experiences during the many seasons when God extended an opportunity to preach. Because of the church teachings I received as a youngster, and my limited understanding of them, I did not respond appropriately. I was correct in stating, "if God wants me to preach, He will have to ask me, not send me a message through someone else." I was not mature enough however, because sometimes God uses others to deliver messages when we are not properly positioned to hear Him *(I Samuel 3)*. Sometimes we both hear and understand Him, we just ignorantly disregard or reject His call. I think I did a lot of each. Chapters 4-6 reveal much of that.

When I talk about *An Electrifying Experience* in Chapter 4, I am by no means suggesting that God shocked me to my senses. In fact, that experience did not wake me up to His voice. What I am saying is that God uses various experiences to reveal His Sovereign ability to protect and preserve our lives, when we could have and should have died from them. One hundred and twenty volts from a normal house plug outlet produces enough current to take someone's life. I jackhammered into 4800 volts and lived to talk about it. My clothing was burned off, but I only had minor burns everywhere else, except on my face. Nobody but a Sovereign God could do that.

Because apprentices usually do the work while journeymen instruct, it could have easily been me that suffered the injuries from the accident with the drum, in Chapter 5. It wasn't that God had anything against Joe that day; He just extended His grace toward me. I certainly didn't deserve it, but He extended it, none the less. That accident, under different circumstances, could have taken my life.

The real estate encounter requires little explanation. I was a legal agent, I had legal rights to be in the house and I had good intentions. That being said, if I had been at any other place in that house when the owner showed up, I probably would have been "dead." At best, I would have been shot. God was ordering my steps even as He is doing now.

I think these experiences finally got my attention. I didn't see them as God calling me to preach, but I did think, "Maybe I need to slow down and take a closer look at my path in life." Why was so much happening? How was I making my decisions, and what was the motivation behind them? The Holy Spirit revealed to me that my life was too noisy. The message to me was, *"You can't hear me because of the noise in your life."* How true that is for so many. We have so many people vying for our attention. When too much information is coming in at the same time, it is equivalent to noise. It was too much to make sense to me. That's where I was. I needed to shut some things down in my life.

I didn't know where to begin. I knew things had gotten out of control, but how to get control again seemed a far reach, I thought. I decided to go back to the one place I had always found comfort. That was in the church setting. I didn't understand at the time that God was even orchestrating that. My biggest problem was feeling like I always had to be in control. It was now time for God to show me that He was, and is, in control of not only my life but also of all things.

Without repeating too much of Chapter 6, let me just refer back to the point when I found myself in front of the church and decided to announce my calling. I began planning what I would say to that body of believers. When that moment arrived, I found myself speechless. All I could say was, *"I've been called to preach."* That's all that needed to be said, but I thought I needed to say something spectacular. That's the problem most of the time with us. We want to grandstand. I was searching for something extraordinary when God wants to take our ordinary and accomplish extraordinary results.

Once I gave God the reins to my life, He showed me that while the call to preach was instant, the development of becoming a preacher was a process. He reminded me that He called me in preparation to preach. He took my mind back to Mark 1:17,

"And Jesus said unto them, Come ye after me, and I will make you to become fishers of men."

Over the years of this process, God had assured me that I didn't need to change my personality. He placed that within me. What I needed to do was change my priorities. He assured me that He would never leave me, fail me, or forsake me. I looked back over the years of these experiences, and He never has. I have learned not only through those experiences but also throughout this journey that God has not, nor will He ever, leave us to our own competencies.

"Being confident of this very thing, that he which hath begun a good work in you will perform it until the day of Jesus Christ:"
Philippians 1:6

As long as we are breathing God's air, we can be confident that He is yet working on us, in us, and through us to accomplish His purposes.

Chapter 8 reminds us that our walk with God is *A Balancing Act*. God has an assignment for each of us, and He desires that we give ourselves fully to it. Nevertheless, He also expects us to be responsible and accountable with the things He entrusts to us, such as:

- Our wives
- Our Children
- Our Jobs
- Our Church family and building
- Our bodies
- Our devotion time
- Our ministry work

All of these contribute to our growth and development. They also create balance in our walk and life.

"But if any man does not provide for his own, and especially for those of his own house, he hath denied the faith, and is worse than an unbeliever." I Timothy 5:8

"And let us not be weary in well doing: for in due season we shall reap, if we faint not. As we have therefore opportunity, let us do

good, unto all men, especially unto them who are of the household of faith." Galatians 6:9-10

God compels us to give our time, talent and treasure, but He wants us to use appropriate balance in doing so. Being souled out doesn't mean you have to sell anyone else out or neglect them. Again, it's *A Balancing Act*.

Chapter 9 introduced the concept of helicopters and airplanes. I shared their differences and their similarities. I don't need to go over those again, but I will say this. One similarity they have is both vehicles were created to take people to a higher height. The helicopter has the ability to instantly elevate upward. The airplane requires a runway and must build up speed to climb. They are designed differently, have different capabilities and different missions, but they perform their missions utilizing their ability to elevate.

God has designed us in similar fashion. We are ground creatures. As a matter of fact, we were created from dust of the ground. That is not, however, where God wants us to settle. God has given us dimension over all His creation. We are to spread the gospel and make disciples wherever He leads us. That may take us to some valleys, mountains, rivers, and even to other continents.

"You ordained him to govern the works of Your hands, to nurture

the offspring of Your divine imagination; You placed everything on earth beneath his feet:" Psalm 8:6

Chapter 10 reflects the period of my life that brought about the greatest transformation. As far back as I can remember, I have struggled with injustices. It seemed like everywhere I looked, I could see some form of injustice being inflicted. I have always been troubled by it, even when it's not directed towards me. I have seen and experienced it politically, racially, socially, economically, in gender and age issues, and unfortunately, I've seen it rear its ugly head even in some churches.

Many times I would speak out against it and would be told that I was too sensitive. Maybe I am, but I don't think that excuses the behavior. Let me assure you that I have not always been on the right side of justice, but my "too sensitive" nature would always convict me when I found myself on the wrong side. I was taught early on that I could have anything I wanted in life if I worked hard enough for it. That is often said but not always true. If you don't fit in (acquiesce), people will often get rid of you if they can.

I detailed this activity in Chapter 10, so I won't expound any further. I will say that I lost several positions during my working years because I wouldn't play the political game. I was offended by the removal, but I will never regret the position I took. My conscience is clear and I can live with my decisions.

In this world I expect injustice to occur because one rule of engagement is often aggression. Get, before you're gotten. Take, before they take from you. I'm getting mine, you better get yours. It's no wonder there is so much friction and battle for the top positions. Ironically, once you're there, you find a bigger target on your back and a lot more villains aiming at you.

I don't know if it was a heart of compassion or a head of naivety, but I've never been the kind of person that tears others down to advance myself. That may be the traditional way to advance in life, but it hasn't worked for me. I needed to find the best way in "Processing It All" if I was going to survive. Again, I went to my rock. God has never failed to put me on the right path.

"Blessed is the man that doesn't walk in the counsel of the ungodly, doesn't stand in the way of sinners, and does not sit in the seat of the scornful. But his delight is in the law of the LORD; and in his law, he meditates day and night. And he shall be like a tree planted by the rivers of water, that will bring forth his fruit in his season; his leaf also shall not wither; and whatsoever he doeth shall prosper." Psalm 1:1-3

After reading and meditating on this passage, I began my souled out journey. Sometimes I think about the attempts made over the years to derail me. Many of those people have left the scene or have become fellow laborers of the gospel. They don't have to answer to me; they have to answer to God, just as I do and all mankind does. Paul says at Philippians 2:10-11,

"That at the name of Jesus every knee should bow, of things in heaven, and things in earth, and things under the earth; And that every tongue should confess that Jesus Christ is Lord, to the glory of God the Father."

I grew to understand that God sometimes uses obstacles to strengthen and transform us. Listen to Paul below,

"And he said unto me, My grace is sufficient for thee: for my strength is made perfect in weakness. Most gladly therefore will I rather glory in my infirmities, that the power of Christ may rest upon me." II Corinthians 12:9

Then the Holy Spirit took my attention to *Romans 12:1-2*. If this doesn't produce a souled out mentality, maybe nothing will. Paul strongly urges us with these words,

"Brothers and sisters, in light of all I have shared with you about God's mercies, I urge you to offer your bodies as a living and holy sacrifice to God, a sacred offering that brings Him pleasure; this is your reasonable, essential worship. Do not allow this world to mold you in its own image. Instead, be transformed from the inside out by renewing your mind. As a result, you will be

able to discern what God wills and whatever God finds good, pleasing, and complete."

In 2004, John Hamburg produced a film titled, *Along Came Polly*. I gleaned several "one-liners" from this movie. One of them that I really cherish was stated by Bob Dishy (Ruben's father) to Ruben's friend, Phillip Seymour Hoffman (Sandy Lyle). Sandy was a guy caught up on being someone of importance and successful in theatre, when all the while his life was passing him by. Ruben's father told him (*I'm paraphrasing*) "It's not about what happened in the past or what might happen in the future, *It's All About The Journey*." That's what I've discovered. It's unfortunate that it took me so long to realize it, but it is true in all developmental aspects of life. There's always a new lesson to be learned, or a new challenge to embark upon, but how we get there is what matters most.

That concept has impacted my approach, walk, focus, and commitment to my calling. Every milestone we reach in life includes experiences that far outweigh the status. I shared all of the experiences from Chapter 1-11 to provide a basis or framework to convey with greater understanding, *why I'm souled out* for the Lord.

Insanity has been defined as "doing the same things the same way and expecting different results. That's where I was for a number of years. I have discovered that I was not alone in that dubious distinction. I thank God that I am no longer in that category.

Getting out was not my doing, but it was my desire. Psalms 37:4-5 assures us that if we,

> *"Take delight in the L*ORD*, and He will give you your heart's desires. Commit your way to the L*ORD*; trust in Him, and He will act on your behalf."*

I mentioned in an earlier chapter that the world is currently challenged with a coronavirus, and at this point, no cure or approved vaccine has been produced. I found a vaccine in Jesus, and He has kept me through dangers seen and unseen. Only God knows whether I get through this one or not. So far millions of people have been infected hundreds of thousands have died from complications associated with it. I have adhered to the guidelines and recommendations and have remained healthy for one reason: God's mercy and grace.

At a time like this, every believer should strive to develop and maintain as close of a relationship with God as possible. God protects His people as He protects His purpose and will. If there was ever a time to know your purpose and be about it, it is now. Please don't hear me saying that any believer that died from this virus did so because they didn't know their purpose. Nor am I suggesting that they were not fulfilling their purpose. What I am saying is that if you don't know it and/or are not fulfilling it, the risk of losing your opportunity to fulfill it seems greater.

Allow me to wrap up by making a few points. Pride, rebellion, and ignorance led to most, if not all of my struggles. Those behaviors, coupled with haste, became a destructive formula; haste makes waste! I'm reminded of the acronym PUSH, pray until something happens. Prayer invites God to –

1. push things forward to accomplish His will
2. Push things back to prevent us from destroying ourselves.

Either way, we benefit from prayer, but we must however be patient enough to wait for God's direction. I was told as a youngster that prayer is talking to God. I learned as I matured that prayer is communicating with God. Communication is a two-way conversation. As Isaiah reminds us,

"But they that wait upon the LORD shall renew their strength; they shall mount up with wings as eagles; they shall run, and not be weary; and they shall walk, and not faint."

Isaiah 40:31

We must wait on the Lord's counsel for guidance and understanding. Isaiah 6:1 conveys a salient point. He says,

"In the year that king Uzziah died I saw also the LORD sitting upon a throne, high and lifted up, and his train filled the temple."

Up until this point, Isaiah did not see God in the fullness of His majesty. Something happened in the year that King Uzziah died that provided a greater view of God. Sometimes, something has to die in our lives to see God for who He is. I call it the magnifying glass concept. A magnifying glass doesn't make things larger; it makes the object appear larger. That's what I got when I souled out for the Lord. I saw God's hands in every aspect of my life, but in a larger way. I didn't need to make God bigger. He is as big as He is. I just needed to adopt a bigger concept of God. I think my trip to the Holy Land facilitated greater appreciation for what our Lord did for us. It also inspired me to give more of myself.

Maslow's Hierarchy of Needs suggests that we develop properly when 5 needs are met. In priority, they are:

1. *Self-Actualization* — Micah 6:8
2. *Esteem* — I Peter 5:6
3. *Love, Belonging/Appreciation* — Jeremiah 31:3
4. *Safety* — Psalms 46
5. *Physiological* — Matthew 6:33

God meets all of these needs and more. As my understanding grew, our relationship developed. As our relationship continued to intensify, a real intimacy was created. Within that intimacy I found -

- *Stability - stable endurance.* -Isaiah 33:6
- *Strength – Power and toughness* -Nehemiah 8:10
- *Sensitivity – Consideration and responsiveness* -Titus 3:2

- *Sensibility – Empathy, discernment and Appreciation -Hebrews 10:34-36*
- *Serenity – Peace, calm and tranquility - John 16:33*
- *Security – Protection, precaution and provision -Psalm 59:9*

When I think of the Lord's goodness and all He is to me, how could I not be souled out for Him? As David said,

"Through my whole life (young and old), I have never witnessed God forsaking those who do right, nor have I seen their children begging for crumbs," Psalm 37:25.

As I said once or twice before, a souled out servant isn't an extraordinary person. He's an ordinary servant yielding extraordinary results because he understands that fulfilling his purpose is totally dependent on God and a totally submitted surrender to His will. That's *Why I'm Souled Out*. I'm not alone. Take a look on the following page at the lyrics of the song, "Souled Out", written by Hezekiah Walker.

Souled *Out*

I am souled out, my mind is made up
I am souled out, my mind is made up
I am souled out, my mind is made up
I am souled out; my mind is made up
　Who can separate us from the love Jesus
Not death, nor life
　Jesus paid the price, now I'm free from sin

　I am souled out, my mind is made up
　I am souled out, my mind is made up
　I've come through the fire, I've come through the rain
　But God, he never left my side,
He's my comfort through all hurt and pain

　I am souled out
　I am souled out
　I am souled out
　I am souled out
　I am souled out
　I am souled out

　My heart is fixed, my mind's made up
　No room, no vacancies, I'm all filled up
　His Spirit lives in me
　And that's the reason, I'm souled out
　Yes, yes, yes, yes

Acknowledgements

Writing a book that reveals my personal experiences in life has been quite challenging. That's probably why I put it off for six years. Candidness, honesty, and transparency, expose faults, failures, and shortcomings, and they can reveal a measure of vulnerability. I thank God for placing a contingent of supporting people in my path. Without them, this work may have never been written.

I'm extremely grateful for my wife, Janice, who has supported my passion for servanthood and allowed me the space, time, and privacy to devote countless hours to completing this work. I'm also thankful for my family, immediate and extended. Their support over the years has been very encouraging. Each of them, in their own, unique way, has provided me the opportunity to demonstrate service to God and His people in ways that some may think as foolish. I thank them for remaining supportive during my obstinate years of development. I'm sure at times, it was challenging. I praise God that you were able to see what others couldn't, a souled out servant of God.

Although pushed to the edge at times, I am thankful for the

challenging times I encountered working with all of the journeymen at General Motors. I learned more than you may ever know. You not only helped me develop my craft, but also impacted all aspects of my life. So many people have benefited, from the skills you taught me.

I am eternally grateful for all of the pastors and ministers, young and old, that poured into my life, from Pontiac/Detroit, MI to Fort Wayne, IN, to Chattanooga, TN. Many of them saw more in me than I was able to see in myself. I thank God for Minister Michael Harris who befriended me like Jonathan befriended David. You didn't know it, but you were just what I needed at that season in my life. I am especially thankful for Pastor Eric Burr and Pastor Jake Gaines Jr. Pastor Burr, you taught me humility. You trusted me, gave me responsibilities, and exposed me to so many great men of God, one of whom was Jake Gaines. I may never have written a book had it not been for his consistent encouragement to write.

My greatest accolade is reserved for my current pastor, Pastor Ternae Jordan Sr. My prayer, my plan and my desire after retirement were not to find a church to pastor but to find a pastor that I could help in growing and building his church. I believed Psalm 37:4, but I remembered Proverbs 16:9. God decided to give me the desires of my heart, and He couldn't have connected me with a nobler person.

I know God's hand was in it because we were not planning to relocate in this area, but God. Pastor Jordan, you have caused God's richest blessing to flow through me, to my family, and to so many people that I have met through you. You introduced me to the Tennessee Baptist Association where I met Pastor Dennis Culbreth (Director of Missions) and Pastor Willie McLaurin (Executive Committee VP). Dennis, you have enabled me to facilitate and complete unbelievable projects and you have blessed many people that you may never meet. Willie, you brought to fruition one of my life's greatest aspirations which was to visit the Holy Land. That great group of travel companions that you assembled and the relationships we developed while traveling will forever be in my heart. Pastor Jordan, I appreciate our unique relationship and all the opportunities that you have provided me. Our bond will never be broken.

To my Senior Editor, Ray Glandon. You have not only been an editor, you have been and always will be my friend. You, my friend, have skillfully transformed my words on paper into a form of art. Your wise counsel is very much appreciated and always right on point. Words cannot express my level of thankfulness and appreciation for you.

Lastly, to my publisher, Steven Lawrence Hill Sr, I thank you my brother for your patience, your guidance, and your suggestions. ASA Publishing Corporation has been a blessing in my life. This is our third book together and you have made this arduous process more manageable each time. May God continue to bless you and your business.

Appendix

Bible versions of scriptures used within this book
- Amplified
- Easy to Read
- God's Word
- Good News
- Holman Christian
- King James
- The Message
- The Voice
- Tree of Life

References
- John MacArthur - Twelve Ordinary Men
- Andy Stanley – The Principle of the Path
- Movie – Along Came Polly
- Steve Jevans – The Children of Israel

www.ingramcontent.com/pod-product-compliance
Lightning Source LLC
Chambersburg PA
CBHW070641050426
42451CB00008B/249